EMOTIONAL INTELLIGENCE 101

By

CLIVE WOLFE
DANIEL SHEPHERD
TOM WALLACES

© Copyright 2018 - **All rights reserved.**

The content contained within this book may not be reproduced, duplicated or transmitted without direct written permission from the author or the publisher.

Under no circumstances will any blame or legal responsibility be held against the publisher, or author, for any damages, reparation, or monetary loss due to the information contained within this book. Either directly or indirectly.

Legal Notice:

This book is copyright protected. This book is only for personal use. You cannot amend, distribute, sell, use, quote or paraphrase any part, or the content within this book, without the consent of the author or publisher.

Disclaimer Notice:

Please note the information contained within this document is for educational and entertainment purposes only. All effort has been executed to present accurate, up to date, and reliable, complete information. No warranties of any kind are declared or implied. Readers acknowledge that the author is not engaging in the rendering of legal, financial, medical or professional advice. The content within this book has been derived from various sources. Please consult a licensed professional before attempting any techniques outlined in this book.

By reading this document, the reader agrees that under no circumstances is the author responsible for any losses, direct or indirect, which are incurred as a result of the use of information contained within this document, including, but not limited to, — errors, omissions, or inaccuracies.

Contents

Anger Management 101 For Men & Women

Introduction 1

Chapter 1: The Reaction of Our Body When We Feel Angry 5

    The Busy Body 6

        Glands 6

        Hormones 7

        Brain 8

        Heart and Body 10

Chapter 2: Stress Management 13

    Major Causes of Stress 16

Chapter 3: Anger in Childhood 22

    Emotional Development in Children 22

    How to Deal with an Angry Child 30

    Dealing with Angry Teenagers 34

Chapter 4: Different Types of Anger................**39**

    Painful Emotions..39

Chapter 5: Is Anger the Same for Men and Women?
....**52**

    Neural Wiring in Men and Women 52

    Hormonal Differences in Men and Women........56

    Social Differences in Men and Women...............60

Chapter 6: Identifying Anger Issues **63**

    Self-Harming 65

    Road Rage..68

    Where to get help for Anger Management 76

Chapter 7: Lifestyle Changes **78**

    Dietary Needs 78

    Exercise..81

    Sleep 83

Chapter 8: Anger Management Techniques & Exercises..**91**

    Help from Others..91

    Self Help..96

Chapter 9: Domestic Violence 110

   Poverty and Familial Violence 110

   Causes of Anger in Relationships 113

Chapter 10: Manipulation and Anger 123

   Narcissistic Personality Disorder (NPD) 124

Chapter 11: The Importance of Empathy 132

   Empathic Anger Management (EAM) 133

Chapter 12: There is a Good Side to Anger 142

   Turn Your Anger Into a Useful Tool 142

Chapter 13: Becoming a Good person 150

   Forgiveness 152

   Sacrifice 154

   Being Non-judgmental 156

Chapter 14: Maintaining Equilibrium in your Life 158

   Alternative Responding Mechanisms. 160

   Don't be a quitter! 163

Chapter 15: Natural Healing 166

Conclusion 172

Cognitive Behavioral Therapy

Introduction 179

Chapter 1: Your Thought Process 183

    Types of thinking 184

        Perceptual thinking 184

        Conceptual thinking 184

        Reflective thinking 184

        Creative thinking 185

        Critical thinking 186

        Non-directed thinking 186

    Development of Thinking 188

    Thinking tools 191

    Automatic Intrusive Thoughts 193

    The Voices in your Head 199

    How changing your thought process can change your life 204

Chapter 2: What is Cognitive Behavioral Therapy? 210

Cognitive therapy 213

Behavior therapy 213

How to go about getting CBT? 214

History of CBT 217

Types of CBT 219

    Brief cognitive behavioral therapy or BCBT .. 220

    Cognitive-emotional behavioral therapy or CEBT 221

    Structure cognitive behavioral training or SCBT 221

    Moral reconation therapy 222

    Stress inoculation training 222

    Mindfulness-based cognitive behavioral therapy 223

    Unified protocol 224

Pros and Cons of CBT 224

Differences between CBT and other psychotherapies: 227

Chapter 3: Cognitive Distortion Awareness 228

What are cognitive disorders? 228

Symptoms of cognitive disorders 229

Effects of cognitive disorders 231

    Treatment 231

Common cognitive distortions 234

Chapter 4: Cognitive Restructuring 239

Chapter 5: Depression & Anxiety 243

Depression 243

Symptoms of depression 245

Types of depression 246

Causes of depression 249

Treatments for depression 250

Anxiety 252

Causes of anxiety: 253

Chapter 6: Journaling 256

Tips for journaling: 260

Does journaling help to treat depression? 263

Gratitude 266

Benefits of journaling: 266

Precautions while journaling: 268

Chapter 7: Mindfulness Meditation 270
Mindfulness-integrated Cognitive Behavior Therapy 273

Chapter 8: Dealing with Negative Thinking and Self-Talk 278
Types of negative thinking: 280

Effect of negative thinking: 282

Changing your belief system 283

How to stop negative thoughts and negative self-talk 285

Chapter 9: Reducing Stress 288
Symptoms of stress: 289

Benefits of CBT for stress: 291

How to make your life less stressful? 294

Chapter 10: Hypnotherapy 297
Misconceptions about Hypnotherapy: 301

Chapter 11: Focusing on the Future 304
Getting Rid of Toxic Connections 304

How to let go of the past and build the new you? 315

    How to stay positive every day?........................ 322

    Quick Fix Tips to stay Positive 324

    Relapse 331

Chapter 12: Precautions 332

Conclusion 336

ANGER MANAGEMENT 101

FOR MEN & WOMEN

By

CLIVE WOLFE

INTRODUCTION

Are you in denial of your anger outbursts?

Anger is not unique to specific people; it's something we all feel from time to time. That's because it's a normal emotion to experience. For some, an angry outburst may be linked to stress and frustration. When anger becomes aggressive or violent, it becomes a problem. If this sounds like you or someone you know, then this book will help you. You will learn to help yourself or someone you know on how to take control of uncontrolled anger.

This is a guide to show you how an aggressively angry person can successfully turn their life around. Aggression is not something we inherit by nature, but it's linked to certain experiences that happen to us throughout our lives. If you can identify your trigger points, then you can begin to heal yourself. Note the phrase "heal." The psychologist's bible, The Diagnostic and Statistical Manual of Mental Disorders (DSM) has an entry for uncontrolled anger bursts. They call it

Intermittent explosive disorder (IED), and it's a recognized psychological illness.

It is easy to understand how those of us who are victims of bad or no parenting can end up with psychological issues. Not that everyone can use that as an excuse for bad behavior, but sadly, studies do link poor parenting with maladaptive behavior in adults. Of course, some have the fortitude and strength of character to rise above an unhappy childhood. However, most will suffer some consequences and often that can show as uncontrollable anger.

This is a book that will guide you on how to turn negative thought patterns into positive ones and how to gain a mindset that can, and will, lead you on the road to success. Success can be measured in many ways. For those who have lost loving relationships through their violent behavior, their triumph will be in rebuilding such social connections.

Allow us to show you how to find your place in society; it's a place that's hidden because of your anger issues.

The knowledge you will acquire in this book will open your eyes. There is so much you can't see just because you are blinded with a negative thinking pattern. Everyone is capable of becoming a better person. For you, it will be defined by a renewed understanding of life.

Learn how to see arguments from others' perspective. We will show you how to change your personality from cold and frightening to warm and friendly.

If you're the victim of an aggressively angry person, learn how to help them. Show them how to rid themselves of the bad and ugly thoughts that riddle them with distress. It can be done through professional therapy or using our self-help guide. Such people need to learn about who they are and how they play a vital role in this world.

Now is the time for action!

No one wants to live a lonely life because of uncontrollable anger. Once you read the contents of these pages, you will know the new direction your life must take.

Many of the ideas in this book are based on long-term studies that have proven to be successful in helping to control aggressive reactions. Being known as an angry person can only be detrimental to your very existence. Instead, learn how to show friendship and compassion to those who pass through your life.

Don't waste another day of your life!

Chapter 1

THE REACTION OF OUR BODY WHEN WE FEEL ANGRY

What comes to mind when you think of the word "anger?"

- ❖ Fighting
- ❖ Shouting
- ❖ Pushing and shoving
- ❖ Blood and Tears
- ❖ Abusive language and fast actions
- ❖ Assault

None of these descriptions portray a comfortable situation and often repulse most of us. Yet, the emotion of anger could save your life as it is one of the emotions that can trigger the "fight or flight" response. This natural biological reaction is essential should we find ourselves confronted by danger. Anger is an emotion that can be difficult to control, but it is possible to regulate the outcome of such a powerful feeling.

Emotional regulation is all about science, or rather about biochemicals. If we understand what's going on in our body, we may find that we're more equipped to regulate anger as well as other emotions, such as stress and depression.

We come to understand in adulthood that our thoughts and actions are ruled by the production of hormones. Such chemicals are produced from various glands around our body. They then make their way to the brain.

The Busy Body

Glands

You might ask, "What has anger got to do with my glands?"

If you know what your glands are doing in your body, you will be better able to control the chemical reactions.

These are the hormones that are making you feel angry and stressed.

There are many glands in our body, and they also vary between men and women. For instance, a woman has a gland that helps to trigger milk for her baby. Men have glands that produce testosterone, which triggers hair growth. There are glands that secrete chemicals into our bloodstream and glands that help us secrete sweat.

Hormones

The hormone we produce most of all when stressed is cortisol. Yet, when we're angry, cortisol production decreases. The hormone that increases in production is testosterone, for both males and females. The sudden increase in testosterone gives us a huge increase in energy. Adrenaline is also increased. This provides us with hormonal arousal that can last for days. That's why you can't always calm down after the situation that ignited your anger is over. Often, we remain irritable after an angry phase, such as an argument with someone. We can also find that for a few days, we can't concentrate very well. That's all thanks to our hormonal production from the glands.

Brain

The brain is our main control center, a place most of our nerves are connected to, hence the name "neuro." Within the brain is a network of transmitters, hence they are called neurotransmitters. Imagine them as little nerve-portals. Most of what we experience is processed in the brain, which then sends messages to the rest of our body.

Whilst the brain is a complex organ, it can help if you think of it as a computer system, with sectional areas.

- ❖ There is a part of the brain called the "cortex." This is where our logic and thinking processes happen. It is our strategic center.
- ❖ Another part of the brain is the emotional center, known as the "limbic." This is actually a primitive part of our brain. When we begin to feel anger, we are using the "limbic" section

more than we are using the cortex. That's why you can't think clearly when you are angry.

- ❖ The final section to include in our analysis is a small department within the "limbic" section. In there, you will find a warehouse full of your memories. This is the "amygdala." Some even refer to it as a reptilian feature. It is here where information passes through to go either to the cortex or the limbic. If the "amygdala" senses a strong sense of negative emotion, it sends it directly to the limbic. This means that the information bypasses the logical thinking of the cortex area. There is even a name for this process; it's called the "amygdala hijacking."

We can blame our anger on "amygdala hijacking." This process will trigger hormones and send our metabolic system into override. As the glands start transmitting adrenalin to the brain, the brain is busy redirecting the main blood flow from the gut to the muscles. We now have biochemical changes going on inside our body. Basically, it means our energy is being redirected to our muscles. We're about to explode with inner tension.

Such metabolic changes then start to affect other parts of our body too.

Heart and Body

Two crucial organs in your body are affected by anger, they are the brain and heart. The heart will pump faster. The brain will redirect energy in the bloodstream from the gut to the muscles. Ever got that churning feeling in your gut that something isn't quite right? That's because of the bio-reactions in the heart and brain. This can cause raised blood pressure. Then you will have a higher temperature, and you will need to breath faster for oxygen relief. You may perspire more in those moments and your mind will be sharper for a while, as you deal with your response.

It is all a similar process to when you feel anxious or stressed. Given all that's happening inside your body, you can see why a prolonged course of these metabolic changes could make you unwell. Considering the results of such negative emotions, it's no surprise that the immune system is weakened and you may suffer any of the following:

- ❖ Headaches or possible bad migraines.
- ❖ Digestive upsets that can lead to heartburn or conditions such as Irritable Bowel Syndrome (IBS).
- ❖ High blood pressure, which weakens the circulatory system making you more prone to heart disease or strokes.
- ❖ Surprisingly, you will also be more sensitive to pain, which is the last thing you want if you're forced to fight instead of flight.
- ❖ You are also less able to cope with inflammation in your joints and muscles so you may feel achy.

Anger, just like stress and anxiety, is an emotion. It is an emotion that triggers fear and excitement. As you pass through the unsettled responses of the emotion, you need to learn how to deal with your inner feelings. Only then can you reduce the risk of becoming aggressive or violent.

- ❖ The word anger does not mean the same as the word violence. Anger is an emotion.
- ❖ Violence is not an emotion; it is a reaction.

Why then do some people lose their tempers openly and become violent? Then there are others who consider their anger to be a bad emotion, and so they try to hide it. We all have different coping mechanisms in place.

Let's now leave behind the responses of the body. We will move on to consider at what point in our lives our anger becomes uncontrollable.

Chapter 2

STRESS MANAGEMENT

Emotions

Many of our feelings are based on one or more of the main six emotions we experience on a daily basis:

1. Happiness
2. Surprise
3. Anger
4. Disgust
5. Fear
6. Sadness

Some believe there are more, but our feelings can fall in-between or be a combination of any of these main categories, such as:

- ❖ Confusion could be fear and surprise.
- ❖ Envy could be disgust and anger.
- ❖ Anxiety could fall anywhere but happiness.

Then again, one emotion can stem from the other, such as anger can be a result of fear.

What makes one person happy may fill someone one else with fear, such as skydiving or other high adrenaline sports.

Every thought we have and every sense we feel in our minds are all related to our emotions. It can be difficult to navigate around the constant stream of thoughts in our heads in any one day. That's why you need to learn to take control. This is never truer if you suffer stress every day of your life.

Stress can fall under anger, fear, and even sadness, as it leads us into a depression. It's a strong emotion that can have negative effects on your wellbeing if you suffer for an excessive length of time. If we overindulge in stress, we are more likely to suffer anger. Once again, it results in too much production of stress-related hormones. After all, the natural chemicals in our body have an effect on every cell we produce.

Some researchers believe that we broadcast and receive vibrations from each other. This is carried out through our electrochemical receptors. They theorize that humans generate vibes like an electromagnetic field. It's no surprise then, how fear can spread like wildfire as a wave of panic through a group of people. Likewise, stress and anger can be passed among the members of a family.

Yet, it is such emotions that help us survive. Anger is a call to defend ourselves. Stress is closely related. Both of which can cause us harm, if we experience them for too long.

When the chemicals react inside us, they send signals out to our blood cells. It takes only 6 seconds to inform the whole body of a new emotion. If we wish to continue feeling that way, we choose on an unconscious level to prolong the feeling. You'd think that we would only choose good feelings, but some enjoy fear, such as adrenalin junkies.

Major Causes of Stress

A major cause of stress in the US is, surprise surprise, money. We all strive to pay the rent and, bills and put food on the table because these are our fundamental priorities. We need shelter and sustenance to survive. Money is not the only cause of stress; here are a few other top reasons:

- ❖ Financial commitments.
- ❖ Separation from a loved one because of death or divorce.
- ❖ Getting married.
- ❖ Moving home.
- ❖ Illnesses.
- ❖ Difficulties at work.

Then there are environmental factors, such as living with a person who makes you unhappy, particularly if they are violent. Living with constant worry can lead to depression and anxiety.

Common Symptoms of Stress

- ❖ Chest pains or palpitations.

- ❖ Feeling excessively hot or cold, often with shivers.
- ❖ Eating too much for comfort, or not enough because of loss of appetite.
- ❖ High blood pressure, which can lead to heart disease if prolonged.
- ❖ Muscle pains through constant tension.
- ❖ Headaches.
- ❖ Sleeping difficulties.
- ❖ Digestive problems.

If you suffer stress, you are more likely to be snappy and short tempered. Your moods could lead to feeling annoyed and angry with everyone. You may say or do things that you wouldn't normally say, such as shouting at the children. Then you live with the regret afterward. Stress can also lead to the overuse of alcohol or non-prescribed drugs as you seek an escape route. However, all this does is add to your problems.

If this sounds familiar and you are experiencing these symptoms, then it's time to take control. Bring your life back into balance. You can begin with a little self-healing, but you should seek help from others too. As with any lifestyle change, it begins with you.

Here are a few ideas to consider introducing into your life:

❖ If you're drinking too much alcohol, allow yourself to drink it only on certain days of the week. Try and have at least three days when you do not consume any alcohol at all. Drinking excessively can make you lose control, particularly if you have a lower anger threshold. You will lose all inhibitions, and that will only make you more aggressive. There are also effects on the next day, making you will feel lethargic and short-tempered in the morning. This is no good if you need to get to work. Try drinking on your days off, such as the weekend only. If you can't control your intake of alcohol, then do get professional help as soon as possible because things will only get worse. Look online for a local Alcoholics Anonymous (AA) group, or ask at a chemist or clinic for details. There, you will meet other sufferers, and you can come together to help each other.

❖ If you're worried that you're overeating for comfort, write down some meal plans for three meals a day. Include healthy snacks such as peanuts, raisins, yogurts, or fruit. You can eat these in-between meals, so you don't feel hungry. Make a shopping list of the meals and only buy what's on the list. Try not to go down the candy aisle or the bakery area when you're in the superstore. The aroma will tempt you to buy those unhealthy items.

❖ You can also try writing down everything you eat in a day. You might be shocked to see how much comfort eating you're doing.

❖ Doing activities such as the ones suggested here will force you to think about the food you're eating. Often we eat with an automatic urgency giving no thought to what we're putting in our mouths. The next time to you eat something, chew on the food for longer. Try to make the meal last 20 minutes because this is the time it takes the receptors in your brain to know when you are full. Think about the flavors and textures. This will stop automatic eating for the sake of it. Keep the naughty carb treats for only one day in the week. Research "nutrition" online. There is a lot of useful information about which foods are the healthiest.

- ❖ If your finances are in a poor condition, then you must seek help and advice. Swallow your pride and admit that you can't keep up with the bills. If your income doesn't meet your outgoings, then it's time to make cutbacks on things such as energy bills, food, clothing but most importantly, on luxury items, such as phones and computers. Sit down and write down every single bill you have so it's clear in your mind as you look at the figures. See where you can make realistic cutbacks. Contact the companies that you owe money to and explain that you can't afford the present amount and need to cut it down. Put your bills in order of importance, with the roof over your head and your food as a top priority.

❖ As you can see from these suggestions, it's all about thinking clearly and admitting you have a problem. You must look at ways of resolving those problems.

❖ The first person you must care for is yourself. If you are not healthy, then you can't keep your family safe and happy. Try to get more exercise into your life because that costs nothing but can be a great cure for a troubled mind and body. Walks are great stress busters, but not on busy streets. Head to a peaceful place, such as a park. Make sure that every week you're doing something for yourself that you enjoy. We all need a break from the fast pace of life, so give yourself a break to reboot yourself for the rest of the week.

Chapter 3

ANGER IN CHILDHOOD

Emotional Development in Children

We are not born angry. Babies cry for attention, but that is an innate instinct and not anger. At what point in our childhood then does anger manifest itself? We know that babies can feel happy because they laugh. Whilst none of us remember much in the way of our baby years, they are busy years as we soak-in everything that's going on around us.

It's argued that some emotions are innate in babies. These are happiness, disgust, and distress. Babies display these emotions through body posture and facial expressions. Other emotions develop over time and become recognized milestones, as outlined below. Some develop quicker or slower than others, but all are normal in a baby's emotional growth.

Baby Steps

4 months - babies can identify certain facial expressions in the faces that look down at them. If it's a smile, the baby might feel happy and smile back.

6 months – babies will mimic those around them more and more. If there's a baby crying, another baby may cry too. If they hear laughter, they may join in.

8-9 months - babies now recognize their main carer and begin to experience anxiety when they're not around. They are now developing emotions that they begin to find uncomfortable. Some may cry out loud in protest, such as with separation anxiety. Others may simply whimper, not quite sure how to handle the new feelings. This is generally regarded as our first emotional rock.

11-12 months – smiling back at someone who smiles at them is no longer automatic. The baby is now associating which feelings go with which expression. It's a trigger of cognitive processes of working things out for themselves.

15-18 months – emotions can begin to overwhelm a baby as they learn the feelings of frustration. Now they're starting to demonstrate their frustrations, possibly even with tantrums. Is this the beginning of anger?

21-months – this is when they start to make conscious decisions. They might be willing to share their toys, then again they might not. Our personality is starting to shine through.

2 years – now that we know how to playact with our emotions, we might pretend-cry so we can get our own way. At this point, humans begin to experience empathy. If we take our playmates' toy and they cry, we have a good idea what's caused them to cry. What we do about it depends on how our own personality is developing.

Do our anger issues begin as a sort of baby frustration? A baby cries to get attention. If no attention is forthcoming, a baby is likely to become confused and start crying louder. Is this the festering of our uncontrollable emotions taking over? What we experience around us at a young age molds our personality.

One such study by Brooker et al. in 2014 tested infants aged 6-12 months to examine anger issues in infants. Parents filled in a questionnaire. This was designed to measure the stability of home-life. It enabled them to identify if any of a set of ten stressful life events had occurred within the family. The infants underwent a process to measure how they reacted to a mildly stressful experience.

The initial results were interesting, in that differences between genders became obvious. The boys showed their frustrations sooner than the girls. Each child's reactions were measured and given a low or high anger profile.

At 3 years of age, the parents were given a second questionnaire. Those measured with a high anger profile went on to be more problematic with their behavior. One prevalent factor that high-anger profilers shared was the amount of stress in their home environment. This indicated that early childhood stresses could be a cause of problematic behavior in later development.

Another study highlighted what effect maternal relationships have on infants. Those that have had a better maternal relationship seem to develop fewer psychological problems.

Mental Health Issues in Children

There have been various researches on the behavior of children over the years. Given that anger is an emotion that even an adult finds difficult to control, it can be tenfold for a child. The most important rule any adult can have is not to lose their temper with a child who is throwing a tantrum. They are experiencing an uncontrollable outburst and need help, not hindrance.

Anger issues in children can go hand in hand with certain mental illness conditions:

Obsessive Compulsive Disorders (OCD)

This is when a child suffers anxious moments on a regular basis. It can then lead to the formation of obsessive behavior. Such behavior can easily turn into a ritual in their lives. If they cannot carry out their ritual, they risk becoming over-anxious, which can lead to an outburst of anger.

Attention Deficit Hyperactivity Disorder (ADHD)

This illness affects the ability of a child to focus and concentrate. Their minds become overactive, and it can lead to the child becoming noisy and disruptive. A child with ADHD can also be quite impatient. Unable to wait for their turn in a line, or wait for anything at all, can lead to difficulties with their peers.

Tourette's Syndrome

It's a form of motor and vocal tics, such as fast-blinking eyes or making loud grunting sounds. The more stressed the child becomes, the more tics and louder their noises. As they develop into teenagers, they can become obsessed with words that may offend. Their deviance is the outlet for stress.

Autism

This can slow down a child's natural social development. In turn, that causes difficulties with communicating and learning. Frustration will be quick to set in and can lead to an outburst of outrageous behavior.

Just like medical conditions, anger issues can be connected to a child's environment and experiences:

Dysfunctional Family

What is happening at home plays a large role in a child's development. If they have an unstable home life where little guidance is forthcoming, the child may have not learned what good behavior is. Or, they may have been allowed to get away with anger outbursts because no one cared to control them. It could be the only way they can defend themselves from abusive parents or siblings.

Parental Behavior

This is the most important role model for a child. If the people they love and trust have constant outbursts of shouting or violence, they may believe this is the norm. Equally, if the parents believe in harmful punishments for bad behavior, this may be a cause for poor development.

Neglect

Even a child from a dysfunctional family can be happy if shown guidance by their parents. If a child suffers at the hands of abusive parents or family members, they will most likely develop anger issues that they have to keep internal.

Traumatic Events

Children can suffer Post Traumatic Stress Disorder (PTSD) if they have a bad experience. Once stress and depression set in, the child will become unbalanced emotionally.

If your child is still pre-school age, they may still grow out of the tantrum stage, most especially once they discover their peer groups don't like it. If their angry behavior continues once they start their school education, this is a warning signal. You may find their teachers suggesting a psychological evaluation. Any parent who is having problems with their child's behavior should welcome this invitation. There is no shame in helping your child to cope with the difficulties that life can throw their way.

How to Deal with an Angry Child

At an early age, anger issues tend to be related to frustration. In infants, it could be something as simple as not getting their own way. After all, we see to a baby's every need when they cry, so it makes sense that toddlers don't understand why that should change. They are now experiencing how to deal with the anxieties of life. When an infant displays frustration through anger, they need the help of an adult to guide them through these new confusing emotions.

Most importantly, as their carer, you should:

❖ **Look for the trigger points** so you can plan ahead. Has their usual routine been altered, thus causing them stress? Learn to recognize what is upsetting your child's emotions to the boiling point of an angry outburst. Understanding your child's personality means you can lessen the impact of those trigger points. For example, do they throw tantrums when shopping at the store? Perhaps you can organize a helper when shopping, or take a favorite toy with you to keep them occupied.

❖ **Stay calm.** The last thing a confused and angry child needs is a shouting adult. They need someone around who is on their side, someone who will help them cope with their overwhelming emotions.

❖ **Be persistent.** If you have said they can't have something and that's the reason they're throwing a tantrum, don't give in. You will not be doing them, or yourself, any favors if you do. Children must learn to cope with life and all of its demands. Guide them away from whatever it is they're demanding. For example, if they're stomping their feet on the ground because you refused to let them watch TV, sit down and read a book together. Show them that there's always a way around problems, so they learn to think of this themselves. Help them resolve their frustrations.

❖ **Encourage** good behavior to shine through. Praise your child when they manage to calm down. Let them know that you're praising them because they're working hard to control their emotions.

❖ **Don't use punishments,** such as stopping their TV sessions. Instead, have a set routine whereby your child can go and sit in a particular chair while they calm down. A sort of time out routine for whenever this happens. Don't leave your child alone, though. They need you nearby to help them get through the emotion unscathed.

❖ **Don't try to reason** with a child in the middle of a tantrum. You will not be unable to get through to them until they've managed to calm down. It's not that they're ignoring you. It's more about being unable to balance reasoning when such a powerful emotion as anger sets in.

Don't be afraid to seek help for yourself. It can be a daunting task dealing with a child who experiences many outbursts. Parents are not trained in the skill of parenthood. It's a "learn as you go" type of job. A parent must make decisions as they go along, and they will not always get them right. Sadly, not all children have good role models in their parents. Their angry outbursts at school could be a mimicking of behavior they've witnessed at home.

There is also the possibility of a medical issue which may be exacerbating the problem. We brushed upon possible mental health problems earlier in this chapter. It's important to address such difficulties as soon as they're recognized. It can become much more difficult to resolve if such behavior continues into their teenage years. The underlying problems could have been there for years, such as bipolar disorder. Untreated, this could lead to anti-social behavior as the uncontrolled conduct escalates.

If your child is repeatedly showing uncontrollable signs of anger and you feel unable to help them, it's time to seek professional help. There's no shame in asking for help. It means that the quality of your child's life can improve. Underlying conditions, such as dyslexia or autism, can make the issues more problematic. It's far better to have a diagnosis at a young age so they can enter adulthood with an understanding of their own condition.

Dealing with Angry Teenagers

A teenager's body is in a constant state of flux most of the time. This can be due to changes to the brain and hormone imbalance. At this age, we often feel almost in a state of alienation from society, as we battle to find our identity. Hormonal changes can begin as early as 7 years of age.

As well as causing acne and hair growth on their bodies, such changes can also lead to wild mood swings. For the youngster whose life has been hindered with bad experiences as well, this is almost certainly going to lead to low esteem levels. Such youngsters will be prone to depression and anger outbursts.

As with adults, the best way to overcome these personal anger problems is with lots of support. Those with a stable family background will most likely scrape through their teenage years unharmed. They will come through as healthy well-balanced grown-ups. Whilst those from broken families may develop mental health issues that can turn them into problematic adults. These are the youngsters who need the most guidance to get through into adulthood with some degree of normality. Such teenagers probably make-up the majority of all angry adults.

Most children will act out certain characteristic traits based on what they've witnessed in their role models. Usually, this is the parents or primary caregivers. It's important as a parent to be aware of this and set a good example. Don't show too much aggression yourself in the home; it really isn't good for the children.

As a parent, if you can reflect on your own teenage years, you will remember how influential your peer groups were. These are important years for forming friendships. At the same time, it's also a time to develop their own incivility. The parents have a lot on their hands and will need to have much in the way of "patience."

Typical teenage behavior can involve eating everything in the refrigerator or being rude to family members, plus many more antisocial tendencies. Loss of temper may result in the banging of doors and disobedience of family rules. To be fair to these mini-adults, they have a lot to contend with:

- ❖ Grueling study and sitting exams can cause terrible worry.
- ❖ Embarking on romantic relationships and finding their niche within their peer group.

They have not yet developed the maturity to deal with these often emotionally-taxing problems. The problems pound at them on a daily basis with seemingly no rest period. No longer do they see their parents as their confidante. In fact, it's often a time of rebellion against their parents and their values.

Parents must be willing to negotiate and compromise. The teenagers will not be looking to compromise on their new-found vivacity for life and independence. Instead, they will expect everything to go their way. Whatever rules you lay down as a parent of teenagers, always leave a way out for them. Don't back them into corners, because they will bite. They are still your children and deserve your love and admiration for the things they do manage to achieve, such as getting out of bed on a morning. It is true that teenagers need more sleep than at any other age.

These are only the rules for a well-balanced family. For teenagers who come from families where their parents can't wait for them to leave home, there lays an even bigger problem. If you are a teenager with unhappy family relationships, seek the help of other adults in your life. Look to teachers, or even visit your doctor to get help with any depression that might be building up.

Keep yourself occupied and learn as much as you can. Knowledge will help you move on once you're old enough and become independent.

Dealing with angry teenagers is as difficult as dealing with an angry adult. It should be dealt with in the same way. Angry people need help if their anger is uncontrollable. They don't need pity; they need a guiding hand and small push in the right direction.

Chapter 4

DIFFERENT TYPES OF ANGER

Painful Emotions

It's important to have an understanding of what causes an angry outburst in the first place. There are different types of frustrations and rage, and they can build up in our minds until we're fit to burst. How we deal with them depends on our own personality and upbringing.

Anger is emotional pain; that's why it comes under the heading of mental health. The health of our mind is key to resolving the symptoms you might feel in an angry flair-up.

Stages of an Angry Outburst

Let's have a look at how a flair-up might play out.

- ❖ Initially, you might feel angry through frustration, rejection, loss, or annoyance. This will be targeted at someone or something that has happened. These are negative emotions that we can all feel inside.

❖ Once psyched up, the hormones begin to play their part. That's when some of us start to lose control. Sometimes that pain is then directed at someone else. Or, we direct it at ourselves and cause even more mental health harm.

❖ When the anger is in full swing, it overrides the painful emotion that triggered it. Now, we almost feel as if we will burst out to find a sense of release to the build-up of anger.

❖ As the anger builds, so too the sense of power and self-defense. This is when you could start to direct negative words at the target of your anger. That aggressiveness can then lead on to being confrontational and violent.

❖ There is a strong sense to seek revenge, or punishment, or to hurt those who instigated the pain in the first place.

Anger Threshold

Every one of us has a different anger threshold and different ways of projecting our anger. Often this can be:

❖ Withdrawing

Looking calm on the outside but withdrawing inside yourself while the feeling passes. Withholding your emotions can be harmful because you have no outlet. It may take a long time before you feel calm again.

❖ Becoming Loud

This could manifest as shouting abusive words and becoming argumentative or feeling a need to lash out at everyone and everything.

❖ Always angry

Life is one big struggle because everyone is against you. The system is against you, and no one ever wants to help. On the contrary, they only want what is yours. Some call a person with this type of anger as someone who has a "chip on their shoulder."

❖ In Denial

Such people don't or won't admit that they have become angry. Nothing is ever resolved because there is no problem in the first place.

Research suggests that on average, each person gets angry at least once a day. Yet they may experience a small annoyance at least three times a day. If the annoyances are well managed, then your body will not suffer from the annoyance turning into anger.

Another problem with showing your anger is that it can have a domino effect. Those around you may get angry back at you. That's because anger is a natural part of self-preservation. It becomes a problem when a person uses it as their everyday way to express themselves. Such people are not only angry with themselves but with everyone who passes through their lives. They struggle to fit into their social surroundings, such as holding a job down or even having a relationship.

Six Dimensions of Anger

A study conducted in 2008 argued that there are six dimensions to how anger can be directed.

1. Reflective or Deflective

Reflected anger is generally in response to some source of provocation. It is retaliatory in nature. This type of anger can run out of control as each player increases their retaliatory action.

Deflection is completely different. This doesn't even need any provocation. Often, the victims are innocent of any wrongdoing. They become the target as the angry person instinctively shifts the blame. The aggressor cannot see how they themselves have done anything wrong. Indeed, they see themselves as the victim.

2. Internal or external

Not all anger is directed at a third party.

Internal anger is withheld and controlled, so others cannot see it. The angry person may be seething within but doesn't wish to reveal their true feelings. They may even feel the need to spare someone the hurtfulness that an angry outburst can cause. Other reasons for internalized anger can have more sinister motives. It's held in check until the perfect moment arrives to exact revenge. Then, it's released with precise planning, so there are no repercussions to the aggressor.

External anger is the process of projecting your anger on others, most often in response to offensive stimuli. The stronger the anger, the more likely the aggressor is to present it in an external fashion. Externalized anger can show itself in various ways, from facial expressions to verbal utterances or sometimes even in the physical form of aggressive mannerisms.

3. Resist or Retaliate

When confronted with a situation that invokes anger, we have two options of dealing with it.

One option is to resist anger. This doesn't mean the aggressor does nothing, but they won't show an outward display of aggression. Instead, they may become non-communicative or even defiant. They could convey a sense of detachment from the person who caused their wrath.

Retaliation can result from the trading of insults. This can progress to the exchange of physical blows. It's what's termed in international relations as "Open warfare." This type of response can soon get out of hand and often result in injury.

4. Physical or Verbal Expression

Generally, when we experience anger, our outlet can take one of two forms. These are verbal or non-verbal.

With nonverbal expression, it's not only what we say, but how we say it. Studies on vocal acoustics in angry people show that for many, their voice raises to a higher pitched level. It will be loud in volume, with the use of a fast tempo. Often, it may become littered with abusive words and expletives. Although that's not always the case, some can appear calm. This type of person will be quietly spoken but heap sarcasm onto their target.

Nonverbal or physical communications of anger may not involve violence. It will become most obvious in the facial area. This can be combined with other body postures and gesticulations, such as hand movement and gait. Sometimes, this behavior can lead to more aggressive actions, such as striking, kicking, or pushing.

5. Uncontrolled or Controlled

Controlling anger has interested psychologists and philosophers throughout the ages. To be able to take control of your own anger requires a good deal of thoughtfulness. This will also include a modification of behavior. In essence, it is a reflective process rather than a reflexive one. It's important to understand that controlling anger does not mean it is eliminated. Rather, it is a process of management.

Uncontrolled anger can, in fact, be a psychological problem. It is a topic included in the psychologist's bible, The Diagnostic and Statistical Manual of Mental Disorders, (DSM).

When an angry response is so much out of proportion to the trigger, it is known as Intermittent Explosive Disorder. This uncontrolled display of anger is not always a physical response but can also be vocal in nature.

6. Punitive or Restorative

Our trigger to anger may depend on whether the perpetrator feels any remorse at stirring up our emotions. This is restorative anger, whereby an apology or regret may help to calm us down. It can depend on the severity of the offense that caused the anger, though. Generally, the desire to move on and get over it all is the main motive of restorative anger.

At the other end of the scale is punitive anger. This is where retribution is the driving force. No apology or offer of recompense can salve the anger of the injured party. Their behavior can become almost obsessive in not being willing to forgive or forget. The type of character who cannot accept this will be unable to move on. They may hold a grudge and look to find a means of getting even with the individual who caused their anger.

Intermittent Explosive Disorder IED

We have brushed upon this earlier in the guide, but IED is an impulse control condition. It can result in an aggressive outburst that is out of proportion to the provocation. This is a volatile type of anger and can happen for no clear reason. Following the explosive outburst, the sufferer will feel a great sense of relief. Later, they may also feel shame and guilt at their uncontrollable behavior.

Around 11-16 million Americans may suffer IED at some time in their lives. This is a recognized psychological disorder. Although there has been no gene identified with the behavior, it is believed to pass from parent to child. A child's environment plays a crucial part in their behavioral development. When raised to receive hard physical punishments, some may replicate such behavior as adults. It can show its ugly head when they lose their temper. There is a range of symptoms in the current iteration of DSM.

Research indicates it may be a cause of abnormalities in certain areas of the brain. Scientists believe IED to be linked to the neurotransmitter known as serotonin. Also to the production of the hormone testosterone. These dysfunctional regions include the limbic system. If you recall, this is part of the brain that deals with emotions and memories. It is situated at the prefrontal lobe of the brain, that regulates impulses among other processes.

People with IED are more likely to abuse others. They find themselves involved in social angry situations, such as road rage. This is because they have a low tolerance range. It's a form of emotional detachment in that they have tunnel vision for those few small moments. Sufferers will experience the physical symptoms of their rage. They can suffer any of the typical reactions to stress. This can include palpitations, tightening of the chest, or headache from raised blood pressure.

It is a disorder that can lead to an abusive adult being unable to experience any positive relationships. Typically, they may even abuse their own children, and so the cycle continues.

IED can take hold of a person in other situations too:

- Anyone who experiences trauma and suffers Post-Traumatic Stress Disorder (PTSD).
- Those with Attention Deficit Hyperactivity Disorder (ADHD) can be gripped with IED.
- Individuals who have Bi-polar Disorder can go on to develop IED.

The good side of this condition is that it has been identified as a mental health issue and as such, can be diagnosed and treated. With the right professional help, the sufferer can learn certain management disciplines. These will assist in controlling their angry flare-ups. People who suffer extreme anger outbursts are not necessarily bad people. They are mostly people who have suffered bad experiences, which have affected their personal growth.

Treatments can include:

- Medication
- Individual therapy
- Group therapy
- Family therapy
- Recreational programs
- Rehabilitation admittance, in the form of a Partial Hospitalization Program (PHP)
- Outpatient Appointments include an intensive period of therapy by visiting a clinic for sessions.

Chapter 5

IS ANGER THE SAME FOR MEN AND WOMEN?

Neural Wiring in Men and Women

Research at Southwest Missouri State University (SMSU), in 2010, found differences in anger control between the genders

- ❖ Men felt constricted if they had to hold their anger inside and could not express it whereas women were more comfortable putting anger on hold.
- ❖ Women see anger as a way to release their frustrations, rather than an aggressive outburst. For this reason, they will seek answers to the cause. Such as, if they constantly feel "frustrated" in their marriage, they may seek divorce.

These differences are most likely caused by pressures of expected social behavior of the genders. whereas, it's acceptable for men to show their anger but not for women. Instead, women have learned to re-direct such feelings. The research indicates that women see anger as counter-productive and so direct the emotion elsewhere.

This does not mean that women never get angry because they do. We must take into account all the other evidence we have discussed, such as upbringing and personality development. The research also found that women who hold back angry feelings are more prone to other mental health symptoms. These can include things like depression and anxiety.

Research at Monash University, in 2016, has shown that men do indeed act differently to women when in stressful situations. They tend to rely on a more hostile approach, such as fight or flight. Whereas women have a less aggressive overture towards confrontations. The researchers termed it as, "Tend and Befriend." The team who conducted the study believe this differing attitude is due to the Sex-Determining Region of Y-chromosomes, (SRY) gene. This is a DNA protein that determines our sexual gender.

However, it's not only genes that are responsible for the different ways men and women respond to anger or stress. We also need to look at the brain's physiology and the release of various hormones.

The female brain is 8% smaller than the male brain. Yet women have much better managing strategies than men. Researchers believe this is due to the variations of neural wiring in men and women's brains. The brain has two halves, referred to as hemispheres. For men, the neural wiring is front to back, with little crossing over the two hemispheres. Women have more of a crisscross pattern of neural wiring, that crosses the two hemispheres.

In conclusion, male anger can be explosive whilst for females, it comes to a simmer.

The University of Pennsylvania, School of Medicine, studied effects on the brain, when angry. They showed evidence that the brain acts differently in men and women when it comes to the raw emotion of anger. This was measured by comparing the frontal cortex area of the brain. Most women had larger areas of the Orbital Frontal Cortex (OFC) than men. Their theory is that the larger this area is, the more capable the person will be of taking control of anger. Their logic "kicks-in" quicker, and they will try to diffuse an angry situation.

It's not that women don't feel the emotion of anger, because they do. The difference is they can manage to internalize such thoughts. The result of this can be that their anger leads to stress. That sets off a whole new set of challenges to the health of the sufferer. Again, it is an emotion that triggers hormonal release. If experienced for long periods of time, stress can become a mental health illness in itself.

This study did confirm one other interesting outcome. The differences between men and women are not necessarily just based on social influences. We are a product of our genetic makeup, and that isn't something that we can control.

Scientists have measured other areas of the male and female brains, and the differences continue to show up. It does make you wonder if the sexes are in fact, different species. It brings to mind the book by John Gray, "Men Are from Mars, Women Are from Venus."

Hormonal Differences in Men and Women
The Effects of Testosterone

Testosterone is a hormone that is part of the androgen group. These are chemicals produced in the male testes and in a woman's ovary. Both males and females have androgens, but for women, they are at a much lower level. The major androgen in males is testosterone. This can make a man feel more alert both sexually and physically.

- Low testosterone levels in men not only decrease their libido but can lead to depression. They will become more irritable and lethargic.
- One study indicated that when a woman or child cries, it can reduce testosterone levels in men. A further study by Cambridge University showed that high testosterone levels reduce empathy. The study also indicated the higher the testosterone levels, the more self-centered the person becomes.
- When two people bond in positive affection, their oxytocin hormone levels rise, and testosterone levels drop although sexual activity will increase testosterone levels.
- Dangerous situations can raise testosterone levels.
- Gambling can make testosterone levels rise when on a winning streak. It gives a sense of confidence and power. Done too often and tolerance levels will become affected, so the person increases the activity. If they continue to succeed, it will give a spike of testosterone levels once again. Now the person is hooked and

constantly attempting to gain that feeling of confidence and power.

- ❖ In overweight men, excess fat tissues will increase their estrogen hormone. As a result, it lowers testosterone levels and decreases their sex drive.
- ❖ If you are a father, your testosterone levels will become around 33% lower than before you became a parent. Plus, you will likely have around 25% more oxytocin, the hormone that helps with bonding.
- ❖ One interesting fact about oxytocin is that dogs have it too. When their humans show them affection, their oxytocin levels rise.

Whilst it's true to say that men release around eight times more testosterone than women, it's not the reason why men get angrier. There have been links to a decrease in testosterone levels when men become angry.

The Effects of Estrogen

Anger in women often takes on a different form but not always of a less aggressive nature. Women may use the power of words more when angry. They may spread malicious rumors as they try to find a route to vent the negative emotion of anger. Of course, men can also use the sharp edge of their tongue when angry.

In opposition to testosterone for men, there is estrogen for women. It's produced in the ovaries. Estrogen can also be reproduced by both men and women as fat tissue if overweight.

- ❖ Low levels of estrogen for women can lead to mood swings.
- ❖ Estrogen is low during menstruation and also throughout menopause. These are typically the times when a woman becomes more irritable and is less able to cope with life's ups and downs.
- ❖ A diet of estrogen rich foods, such as flaxseed, nuts, and even red wine, is a natural way to increase this hormone.
- ❖ High levels of estrogen have been connected to breast cancer.

Hormones play a great part in our moods and behavior. These are not the only cause that can lead to mood swings and out of control emotions.

Social Differences in Men and Women

We know that the brain functions differently between the genders. Here are some other differences between the genders that support the fact that males are more aggressive than females:

- ❖ The more obvious differences are in physical appearance. Men are usually taller with broader shoulders. Women often have wider hips and larger breasts for childbirth. Men grow facial hair, and women usually have quite a smooth face with little hair growth. We share the same amount of limbs, and our internal organs are similar, though our bone structure does differ slightly.
- ❖ There is another difference that's not so evident, that of chromosomes. We share 22 of

these that are the same, with another 2 that are different according to gender.

❖ Historically, women have always been seen as the weaker sex, not only in physical strength but also in mental capacity. Of course, we now know that women can be just as intelligent as men, yet society still treats them as the weaker sex. Gender inequality is often at the top of many politicians' agenda. Perhaps one day in the future, all people regardless of their gender or ethnicity will be treated as equals, but we're not there yet.

❖ In one survey, 54% of men believed gender differences were biological. Yet 67% of women believed that it's more of a social problem.

❖ Whilst the workforce is evenly split, men are still considered the main breadwinner. Though this is changing with at least 40% of women becoming the primary breadwinner in their family.

Men tend to be the risk takers, whereas most women tend to be cautious. This could be why statistics show that men are more likely to die from an accident than women.

One researcher at the University of California believes that "The female brain has evolved to avoid physical outbursts. This means that their children are less likely to get hurt."

Does this all fall back to our ancestral behavior when men would hunt and protect, and women banded together to make a home and keep the children safe?

If men were unable to vent their aggression in a physical manner, would they be more likely to evolve with similarities to the female biology of the brain?

One thing is for sure. There are clear biological differences, and these have most likely led to social differences.

Chapter 6

IDENTIFYING ANGER ISSUES

One symptom often seen in someone who loses their control regularly is that they are usually the last person to realize what they've done. That's because they are often in denial and afraid to admit to any such weakness.

To cure this character flaw, they must first be able to admit that they have a problem. As with addiction, it is a mental health issue that can be rectified with help. Though if you cannot admit that you have a problem, then how can you cure it if it doesn't exist in your mind? You have to be ready to make changes in your life.

Broken relationships are often a common problem for those with anger issues, more so if their anger outbursts result in violence.

We know that anger is an emotion, and as such, we can all feel it on the odd occasion. There may be times when we can feel more irritable than normal:

- A woman's menstrual cycle results in unbalanced hormones. This can result in many emotional symptoms, including feeling more irritable.
- Men tend to bottle up their emotions more often than not. This can have a similar effect as a ticking bomb or a pressure cooker. It can explode at any moment.

It's important to understand the symptoms of an anger disorder, so you are aware of the risks. Learn to know your own signs that your emotions are negative.

How often do you feel:

- Irritable
- Anxious
- Stressed
- Annoyed with just about everyone

These are normal emotions to feel on the odd occasion. If you're feeling them on a daily basis, the chances are you'll also lose your temper more often.

Self-Harming

Anger can show its ugly face in many forms. One such form can be self-harming.

- ❖ A person who feels the need to harm themselves is experiencing unsafe thought patterns.
- ❖ They are most likely already suffering from an array of negative emotions, such as anxiety and stress.
- ❖ They tend to blame themselves for every mishap they go through. As they pent up their emotions, there is no outlet. This leads to a feeling of losing control. At this point, they may self-harm to take back some control of their life.
- ❖ It could be that they feel their anger is out of control. By injuring themselves, it will give them focus elsewhere, so the anger subsides.
- ❖ Or, it could be that instead of hitting out at others, they harm themselves.

❖ In a sense, they don't wish to burden others. If someone does attempt to help them, they will feel even more guilty at imposing their problems upon them.
❖ Whilst self-harming makes them feel more in control, the truth is that they are losing control.
❖ They have no coping strategies in place. This makes them feel completely overwhelmed, resulting in negative emotions.
❖ Self-harming may be their own form of punishment.
❖ Or, as anger sets in, they may self-harm on impulse.
❖ Afterward, they may hide the injury through a feeling of shame.
❖ Or, they may seek attention for the injury. By showing someone their pain, they can now accept outside help because there is a plausible reason to do so.

One thing many self-harmers have in common is a self-loathing of themselves, at least at the time, they are harming. This is a common form of expression in the teenage years. Once again, hormonal imbalance is ruling behavior. The body is going through changes from being a child to becoming an adolescent. Sadly, it can go on into adulthood. In general, though, teenagers do learn other ways of coping as they mature and will stop self-harming.

Other forms that anger can present itself might be:

- A lack of patience for others.
- Speaking rudely to people, often without any real reason.
- Blaming other people for everything that is wrong in your life.
- Being sarcastic at another person's expense.
- Threatening other people.
- Raising your voice most of the time.
- Clenching your jaws often.
- Sweaty palms or sticky neckline.
- A feeling that you need to explode, such as shouting and lashing out in an aggressive manner.

If you think these are familiar feelings and you experience them on a daily basis, then it's time to take responsibility and seek help, not only help for yourself but for those around you and your loved ones. You may not realize that you've been taking out your anger on them because you may well be in deep denial.

You're making yourself mentally and physically ill. Those closest to you will also be feeling similar feelings as they see you suffer. They themselves are subject to your wild outbursts of anger.

Road Rage

What is it that can make calm people into monsters when they get behind the wheel of a vehicle? It's such a strange phenomenon!

Passengers in the vehicle don't particularly serve as a buffer. The driver may still rage at other drivers on the road, even with their children present.

Whilst road rage may seem to be a minor problem as we can all lose our tempers when witnessing bad driving, it can have serious consequences.

Road rage is an incident whereby a driver becomes verbally or physically abusive to another driver or pedestrian. Sometimes, it can lead to dangerous driving as they use their vehicle in an aggressive manner. Drivers who act with uncontrollable rage could be suffering from Intermittent Explosive Disorder (IED). The American Automobile Association's studies show that men are the main culprits. They caused 96% of road rage incidents in the past and averaged around the age of 33-years old.

Road rage was a factor in over 400 fatalities on the roads in the USA in 2015. This might seem a low figure, but it is a growing problem. The National Highway Traffic Safety Administration informs us this problem has increased by nearly 500% in the last ten years.

The risk from road rage is not always the fault of other drivers. If you act in this way, it could be you that hurts yourself and your passengers. The loss of anger control will inevitably lead to dangerous driving. Even if it doesn't lead to an accident, your loss of temper is bad for your heart. Your blood pressure will increase, which is a major factor of cardiovascular disease.

Where does a driver's patience go? Is it:

- A need for control?
- A violation of our personal space, which is a much larger area when we're sitting in a car.
- Primitive hormones?
- Lack of intellect?

One thing is for sure; it's a risky business and could easily lead to:

- Accidents
- Arrests and fines
- Assaults
- Families falling out with each other
- Embarrassment
- Lawsuits

With the intense release of hormones comes an increase in stress levels. That's what's happening to make drivers so angry with each other. It doesn't need to be a long journey because it boils down to a lack of compassion and control. Control your angry thoughts and stop blaming everyone else. It doesn't matter who's to blame so long as no one is hurt. Only then will the release of hormones slow down and stop your angry explosion.

One of the major problems is that most drivers expect other drivers to behave as they do. This leads to them feeling offended if someone else's driving habits clash with their own.

Such easily-offended drivers will be busy thinking:

- ❖ Why won't they leave the junction quicker? They're holding everyone up.
- ❖ Why are they driving so slow?
- ❖ How dare they tailgate me?
- ❖ I'm going to make sure I get off first when the traffic signals change color!
- ❖ The cheek of it, they're trying to overtake me. I'm going to speed up!

If you're a regular driver, then these statements may sound familiar to you.

We're all meant to wait for our turn in a fair system. Yet, when traffic's moving slow, we tend to think we're the only ones who are stuck. Or, we are the only ones who are in a rush. Guess what? Everyone has somewhere they need to be; that's why they're on their journey in the first place.

For many, manners can disappear when someone aggravates them. Down goes the window and they shout out at who has offended them, or they make obscene gestures. In reality, all it achieves is making the situation worse.

This is a form of anger that can get most of us hot under the collar, and it isn't good for anyone; victim or perpetrator.

It's so easy to say that the next time it happens, we will deal with it better. The trouble is, our emotions are on overdrive, pun intended.

Here are a few suggestions on how to keep yourself calm whilst sitting in your vehicle:

❖ Don't forget the breathing techniques. Should you feel that anger stirring in the pit of your stomach over some annoyance whilst driving, take that deep breath through your nose. Follow it through as in the relaxation breathing exercises.

❖ It helps if you don't play fast music on the radio while you drive, this can feed your aggression. Instead, play something a little more soothing so you keep your calm should someone annoy you on your journey.

❖ Listen to a podcast, though without earphones on so you can still hear the traffic. This forces your thoughts elsewhere as you listen to the person speaking. Of course, your full concentration needs to be on the road, so it should only be background noise.

❖ Stop traveling everywhere as if you're in a hurry. If you are, then set off earlier and don't get so stressed if traffic holds you up. Good planning should mean you have less urgency. When calculating your timing, you should allow for hiccups along the way. If there are none, then you'll get there earlier.

❖ Don't drive when you're tired. Your mind is foggy, so you're unable to give you full attention to the skill of driving. There are many fatal accidents on the roads caused by drivers falling asleep at the wheel.

❖ If something does happen and you're approached by another driver, swallow your pride and show them a warm smile. Even if it's not your fault, apologize anyway so long as there's no harm done. It takes far more guts to apologize than it does to argue back.

Use all those new skills you are practicing, such as empathy, compromising, and forgiveness. Yes, there are many bad drivers out there, but as a driver, you already know that. If you don't like it, then don't drive. Otherwise, you must learn to put up with the incompetence of other people. If someone's tailgating you, let them past. They clearly haven't read any guides to teach them how to be a calmer individual. They may not be very nice people in the first place, so don't risk harm to yourself, your passengers, or your vehicle.

Even if the other driver has broken the law, don't confront them. If you have a dashcam, then you could go to the police later.

Most of the time, road rage is over nothing much to start with. In many instances, the drivers will have an altercation and then continue on their way. They will still experience the negative vibes of the situation. This, in itself, may cause them to suffer the consequences of the incident for hours afterward. Far better to brush the incident off and accept it's all "par for the course." Sooner or later, you're going to come across a bad driver, accept this as a fact of life.

We all expect people to abide by the rules in our society. Yet, when on the road, reckless drivers disrupt this very system outright. They do things that are unfair and unjust, and we all want to punish them for it. It is far better to ignore such deviant folks and hope they get their comeuppance over their ignorant driving skills.

Sooner or later, they'll do something wrong which might be seen by the police. It's inevitable for such people who drive without care or respect.

Where to get help for Anger Management

One way to find help for your anger issues is to search out any local support groups for anger management. You can do this by enquiring with:

- ❖ A doctor.
- ❖ A chemist in your area.
- ❖ Any health clinic.
- ❖ Online research.

At these groups, you will meet fellow sufferers, people who are going through the same experiences as you. There is no easy solution, and in some ways, it is willpower that will get you through. It will be easier with others helping you through the difficult process. Once you manage to learn how to control your anger, you will become a much happier person, and your family will be happier too.

There's a variety of medications that can help tremendously. Your doctor will need to know about your anger flare-ups and any depression that often goes hand-in-hand with anger.

Admit to yourself that you have a mental health problem. It is not a label, but an illness that's caused by an imbalance in your brain and hormones. That's why medication works so well. Once your hormones are stable, you can then learn coping strategies. By taking such action, you know that you're well on your way to being a better person, not that an angry person is a bad person unless they're hurting others intentionally. It will be worth it as you begin to feel healthier along with your new lifestyle.

Chapter 7

LIFESTYLE CHANGES

You might be thinking that making lifestyle changes is something that someone else would do, not you. Or, that it's something people do when they're recovering from an illness. On top of those thoughts, you most likely believe it's all about money; commercial enterprises are trying to get you to buy their expensive "natural foods" and the latest keep-fit equipment. The truth is that it's none of those scenarios. What it really means is ridding your life of bad habits. It does not need to cost money, but if you don't improve your lifestyle, it will cost you your health.

Dietary Needs

Let's start right at the very basics with the food that you put into your body. What's this got to do with anger management, you ask? You're quite right; this isn't a dietary book. Yet, there is a need to understand how the human body works if you are to make positive changes in your life.

The natural processes that take place in your digestive system are a result of the types of food you choose to put in there. If you eat unhealthily, such as choosing high carbohydrate foods, then your body will suffer the consequences. Such foods are poisonous to the body, and here's why:

- ❖ The gut absorbs foods for nutrients. Healthy foods, such as vegetables and whole-wheat ingredients, break down at a slow rate. This means your body benefits from the rich nutrients. It then passes through into the small intestine. From there, the nutrients enter the bloodstream. Next, they're directed to the pancreas and liver to use up the glucose, vitamins, and proteins.
- ❖ Some foods pass into the bloodstream much quicker, such as carbohydrates. By entering quicker, they don't get broken down and turn into glucose. Too much glucose results in a

spike in blood sugars. The food that has caused a sugar spike then triggers the pancreas to produce insulin. Too much insulin can lead to becoming insulin resistant, known as diabetes type 2.
- ❖ When we have an excess supply of glucose, the body doesn't need it all. Rather than waste it, it is turned into fat and stored away in case we need extra energy at some point. Hence, we now start to put on weight.

This is a simple analogy of how harmful eating high carb foods can be for your body. It's not only diabetes type 2 that can be a consequence of eating unhealthy foods. There are a whole host of bad conditions that come from having too much fat in storage.

- ❖ Being unable to sleep
- ❖ High blood pressure
- ❖ Heart diseases
- ❖ Strokes
- ❖ Certain cancers
- ❖ Liver diseases

- ❖ Kidney diseases
- ❖ Unhealthy bones leading to osteoarthritis

It's a long and worrying list, but it is also an avoidable list of conditions.

Exercise

That dreaded word!

Before you let out a sigh of, "here we go again," bear in mind that we're discussing your health.

We're not talking about jogging for miles until you drop, or even paying extortionate gym fees. It's simply a case of stopping yourself from becoming too sedentary. Exercising regularly can help a lot in regards to keeping your mind clear.

Let's first discuss what happens to your body when you exercise, even just a little. Whether suffering anger issues or not, we should all exercise as recommended by the health authorities.

Avoid Inactivity at all costs!!

Every week, you should do the minimum of medium-intensity exercise for at least 2 hours and 30 minutes throughout the whole week.

That means you can split it into:

- ❖ 5-days x 30-minute sessions.
- ❖ Or, 5 days at 15 minutes on a morning, and 15 minutes during the afternoon.

There is no need for a rigid and painful exercise routine. Depending on your age and circumstances, a brisk walk could fulfill the criteria.

This is not enough exercise to lose weight, but it's enough to keep your heart fairly healthy.

That's why there is a little more besides the medium level of exercise. Don't worry. It only amounts to an extra 1 hour and 15 minutes a week doing a more vigorous exercise regime. You may know this type of exercise as aerobics. It means the exercise should be designed to make your heart pump a little faster, resulting in making you short of breath. Here are a few ideas on how you can achieve this part:

- ❖ Add another 15 minutes to the walks you do already as outlined above, only walk faster, or uphill.
- ❖ 2 x 35-minute swimming sessions a week.
- ❖ 3 x 25-minute sessions of cycling.
- ❖ Get a home rowing machine and row for 15 minutes x 5 days.
- ❖ Start dancing lessons.

In total, it means you should be exercising for around 4 hours in the entire week. That's not a lot of your time!

Sleep

By making simple changes in your lifestyle, such as eating healthy foods and doing the minimal of exercise, your body will start to feel better. This, in turn, will lead to better sleep, and that in itself will help reduce the feelings of irritability.

How much sleep is enough?

It is not a myth; teenagers really do need more sleep. As we enter our teen years, we should be getting around 8-10 hours of sleep. From around 18 years onwards, between 7-9 hours should suffice, depending on your metabolism.

If you don't get the right type and amount of sleep, you will:

- ❖ Be less able to concentrate throughout your waking hours.
- ❖ Have a slower and more ineffective immunity system. This results in catching those annoying bugs and viruses that spread around rapidly and will not help with your mood.
- ❖ Increasing the chances of heart disease, as your heart rate is affected if you don't get enough sleep,
- ❖ Whilst too little sleep is harmful, so too is having too much sleep. A study by researchers at Keele University indicates that those who sleep longer than 8 hours have an increased risk of heart attack and premature death.

❖ Inadequate sleep results in mood swings, which can lead to accidents if you're feeling argumentative. If this happens on a regular basis, it can ruin your quality of life.

American Academy of Sleep Medicine (AASM) informs us that only 1 in 3 adults is getting adequate sleep. That leaves a lot of tired and irritable adults walking around; let's hope you're not one of them.

Remember this easy equation: a healthy diet plus the recommended amount of exercise will equal a good night's sleep. If you feel more refreshed when you wake up, then your mind will be clearer to face the ups and downs of the day ahead. Now that you can concentrate better, you can begin to teach yourself to have more positive thoughts. Push away those negative ones; you don't need them in your life.

This is not an easy thing to do when under stress, or you've had bad experiences in your life. None of these changes are going to be easy, but they are all necessary if you want to bring your anger under control. To be successful in this, you need the right mindset and thinking patterns. That's why it's so critical to get yourself on track with the right diet, exercise, and sleep.

What then is a positive mindset?

First and foremost, it is about changing your own mental attitude and not about making those around you change.

People who display symptoms of aggressive, angry bouts are the most likely to allow their negative thoughts to rule their heads. It can be made worse because of depression or stress. Often it festers because of a bad experience or a difficult relationship. There can be any number of valid reasons that have unbalanced their lives. When the mind is so confused that it causes stress, it's a time to call for help. Self-help is a good way to start. The responsibility lies within ourselves to make these changes in our lives. If you can help yourself, it opens the way for other people to help you too.

We must learn to push away our negative thoughts and replace them with more positive thinking patterns.

This will also involve using and altering our communication skills. If we can communicate better with others, we can learn to understand their point of view. It is a start to learning to use the skill of empathy.

There is a difference between empathy and sympathy, the latter being that you feel sorry, or even pity, someone else. Empathy is not pity. It is being able to put yourself in someone's place and understand how they feel.

Let's look at an example of this.

- ❖ You see someone on the street asking for money.
- ❖ Your first thought could be that they want money for drugs or alcohol. Negative thinking! Then again, you don't want to be naive and ignore such truths.
- ❖ Your second thought could be that they are lazy and should get a job. Negative thinking! You know nothing of how or why they are in the situation they are living. Don't be so judgmental!

Ask yourself why anyone would live that way voluntarily? If you can do this, it means that you're starting to see their situation from their point of view.

Consider a few reasons why they might be in that situation, such as:

- ❖ Are they recently divorced and ended up homeless?
- ❖ If it's a teenager, then it could be that their parents don't care about them. They may not even have any parents to guide them?
- ❖ If it's a woman, she could have been in a violent relationship and ran away from her home to get away from it.

There could be so many reasons why this person finds themselves in the situation they're in.

No one is saying that you have to give them money. It could be that are dependent on drugs or alcohol. It's not unusual for those in such difficult circumstances to follow such a path. If you want to help them, then consider buying them a sandwich or an item of warm clothing. Or simply talk to them, it might be just what they need to feel human again.

The main thing is not to have negative thoughts about others you know nothing about.

The positive way to think is:

- ❖ Not to be judgmental of others.
- ❖ Try to be more empathic of what other people are thinking and experiencing as they too go about their daily toil.
- ❖ Help other people when you can.
- ❖ Don't hold grudges when someone does something wrong to you. All this does is eat away at you, making you feel negative those emotions. Learn to let the grudge go.
- ❖ Be as forgiving as possible. It's not easy, but realize that people do make mistakes. If their errors have an impact on your life, the chances are it was not intentional. Even if it was, learn to rise above pettiness and move on.
- ❖ Behave in an ethical way. Make an attempt to understand others and the reasons they make

mistakes. We return to empathy later because it is such an important skill to learn. You must find the strength to take on some of these challenges. They are not easy by any means. We are all challenged in this world to make the best of our situations.

The next time you feel anger welling up inside, ask yourself questions. Why is that person behaving the way they are? Try to understand the argument or situation from their point of view. Most of all, learn how to ignore the people that you cannot learn to like. It's okay not to like certain people, but learn to shut them out of your own life. If they cross your pathway, let them go by freely. With a positive mindset, you can learn to cope with many difficult people and situations.

In the next chapter, we will look at techniques for helping you to take control of your anger impulses.

Chapter 8

ANGER MANAGEMENT TECHNIQUES & EXERCISES

If you suffer from uncontrollable anger bouts, then you will benefit by learning certain control techniques. Instead of swimming the moat around and around your castle, open up the castle doors and let the help flow in.

Help from Others

One thing you must learn to do is accept help from other people when it's offered. Without others in your life, making changes can be a much more difficult task.

Medication

There are certain drugs that can be very helpful for uncontrollable mood swings. You must speak to a doctor or clinician so they can assess the right medication for your personal situation. As we explained earlier, much of our body is ruled by chemicals called hormones. The right medication can balance out the neurotransmitters in the brain, which in turn allows you to cope with your moods. Neurotransmitters are nerves and cells that are interconnected in the brain. They are triggered into action by the hormones we produce.

Therapy Sessions

You can do this privately or be referred by a doctor. It means attending sessions whereby you can talk about your personal experiences. It's a great opportunity to express your mental health concerns to a professional who can help with diagnosis. You may prefer one-to-one therapy, or go to group sessions, or both. Groups will consist of other people experiencing similar problems. It is a place to share your symptoms and worries. Therapy has proved successful for many with their mental health issues.

The best people to help with any type of mental health problems are the professionals. They are the experts in their field. After many years of studying, they will have a full understanding of the biological processes that cause such problems. Their hard gained knowledge means they know the best procedures on how to relieve relevant symptoms. Here are a few ways the experts can help you with the popular cognitive behavior therapy. Remember though; treatment results vary for each individual.

Communication skills

Angry people who become uncontrollably frustrated may feel as though no one understands their point of view. Whenever they try to put it across, they may become further annoyed as others disagree with them. Their reaction is to block others off and not listen. By improving their own communication skills, they will be better able to get their thoughts across to other people. Our instincts tell us to keep a distance from aggressive situations because they might be a threat to us. So, instead of shouting at others, the aggressor should learn how to get their opinion over in a calm manner. That is all it will take to get other people to listen.

Problem Solving

Many people who have mixed emotions prefer to shut their minds off from problems that come at them. This is a mistake, as rarely do problems resolve themselves, so they're unlikely to go away. When they come back a second time, they're usually even worse. It is far better to learn skills that will help aggressors confront problems in their lives. Sometimes, just being able to collect their thoughts will direct them to look at logical solutions. For instance, debts can be handled with the right guidance. Access to seeing children in a marital breakdown can be handled with the right mindset and professional guidance. Poverty does not mean you have to starve; there are ways of finding access to food banks. There are always solutions if you can get your mind focused on finding and accepting them.

Avoidance

Those of us who suffer low self-esteem prefer to avoid other people and situations, particularly those involving problem-solving. It's important for them to learn how to confront their inner demons. These are often in the form of memories. An aggressive person might feel brave when they're screaming, shouting, and lashing out. All that serves is to show how frustrated they are. Avoidance only puts things off temporarily, so it's vital to learn skills to help you cope.

Humor

They say a smile can make all the difference, and a laugh can turn your life around. There is rarely find anything to laugh at in therapy, but with the right treatment, you will laugh again. With the right kind of help, you will learn that there is another side to life that is not always negative. Sometimes, you can learn to appreciate nature and the world around you, once you realize it's there. Though it's more about learning to think positive thoughts and banish the negative ones. It's not only about learning how to control your anger, but also about learning how to control your emotions. Once you know how to deal with the negative ones, such as sad or disturbing memories, you will become a happier person. Humor can be a great healer.

Self Help

Once you recognize that you have a problem with your emotions, you are halfway on the road to recovery. It takes a strength of character to admit your own weaknesses. There are many who will not. If the symptoms we have discussed in this guide apply to you, then there is a way forward. Recognizing the problem is the first step.

Now you must find the strength to tackle your internal insecurities. We all have them. The best way forward is to turn your life around. For some, the symptoms may not show on the surface, but it doesn't mean they aren't struggling on the inside.

The following self-help exercises have proven to help calm stresses and dampen anger.

Breathing Exercises

This one is so easy that you can do it anywhere, anytime. People who are feeling angry will often breathe rapidly as their anger increases. If you feel this happening, then force yourself to:

- ❖ Take a deep breath through your nose and count to four. Counting in your mind also helps you to concentrate and takes your mind away from the offending incident. Hold that breath for a count of six, and then let it out as if you are pushing out all your fiery emotions.
- ❖ With the second repeat of this breathing technique, as you inhale allow your belly to expand outwards. Your chest will rise a little but try and concentrate the air into your stomach. Hold for a count of six again, and exhale through your mouth.

Repeat this as many times as you need, and the process of the exercise will be a distraction that will help to calm you down. Not only that, but you are increasing the oxygen levels in your bloodstream. This helps to lower blood pressure that would normally build-up with stress.

You can be standing, sitting, or even lying down, if possible. Learn to incorporate this relaxation exercise into your life. It's not only for when you feel you might explode with anger, but it's also a great de-stressor. If you get to take a break and sit down, this exercise will help you wind down for a few moments.

Muscle and Joint Relaxation Exercises

It's better if you can lay down for this exercise, but you can still do a smaller version of it if you're standing or sitting. It's more of a soothing relaxation method, rather than an instant fix. Let's assume something has upset you and you are feeling tense. Walk away from the situation and attempt these relaxation techniques. You'll be so busy concentrating on these exercises that you'll naturally become calmer.

The whole routine can take at least half an hour or longer. If you have time to do the full workout, it incorporates the entire body. If you only have time to perform one or two parts, count to at least ten in your mind before you move between body parts.

❖ Close your eyes if you can, but don't worry if you can't. The main task is to focus for a minute or two until you calm down.

❖ If you are doing the entire workout, then start at the far extremities of your body, your toes. Wiggle them around for a count of 5 seconds. Follow this by squeezing any muscles you can feel in your foot. We're not always aware of foot muscles because it's not something we consciously think about. Be careful not to get a cramp because we don't often give these muscles such attention.

❖ Move your concentration to your ankles. Circle both feet around one way, then circle them around the other way.

❖ Move on to your calves. Squeeze those calf muscles as hard as you can on both legs, then relax and loosen the tense muscle. Do this around 10 times.

❖ Next, move up to the knees. You'll need some room for this exercise, so if space is tight, give it a miss. Bend those knees and then straighten the legs out and do this to both legs 10 times.

- ❖ Now squeeze the thigh muscles underneath, then relax. Repeat at least ten times. Then repeat but squeeze the top of the thighs.

The idea is to work your way through your body. Next could be your buttock cheeks, and then maybe your stomach muscles, chest, shoulders, tops of arms, and the bottom of arms; squeeze each muscle and then relax it to the count of 10 times each.

- ❖ Rotate your shoulders and shrug them up and down. Push them backward, upwards and any which way that you can feel muscles pulling.
- ❖ When you get to the hands, spend some time stretching out your fingers and rotating your wrists around. Squeeze whatever muscles you can feel in your hands but again be careful of cramps.
- ❖ Rotate your neck in full circles one way and then the other. Tense the muscles so you can feel them pulling on your shoulders. This part is a great routine if you have a headache.

- ❖ Finish on your face and open your mouth as wide as you can, pushing your jaw downwards. Pull faces to stretch the facial muscles and the neck tendons. Squeeze your eyes open and shut many times. Do as much as you can to feel all the different muscles in your face that you're normally aware of.
- ❖ Before you open up your eyes again, do those breathing exercises if you have time.

What this entire workout achieves is a total relaxation of all your muscles and joints. It takes some time to do a whole session, but it will leave you feeling good. When you find yourself in a stressful situation, try to sit down and do a small part of it. If you don't want anyone to notice, tense muscles they can't see, such as your thighs. The tensing and relaxing of those muscles will help you to calm down.

Visualizing

This relaxation method can give instant release to tension. It's a good way to calm a rising temper.

❖ Begin with a few deep breaths from the breathing exercise we discussed earlier.

❖ While you're focusing on your breathing regime, start to visualize a pleasant calming place. Perhaps a favorite beach, a woodland, or anywhere else that's peaceful. Don't think about anywhere noisy, such as a football game; the idea is to get your mind into a peaceful place.

❖ Focus on the detail of the imaginary situation you have placed yourself in. Can you hear the sound of the ocean or the wind in the trees? What can you smell, such as the salt of the sea, pine trees, or freshly cut grass? Walk yourself through the scenery as though you were on a path in that place.

❖ It doesn't even have to be a place. You can imagine anything that you personally find pleasant, such as the face of a loved one when they laugh. What are they wearing? What are they saying to you? Or, imagine your dog when he comes running to greet you as you walk through the door. Think about his warm breath and sloppy tongue as he attempts to lick you.

~ Or it can be an object, such as a plain box whereby you open the lid and watch a red line of steam that goes into the box. That steam represents your temper as it's leaving you. Allow it to come out of and then watch it enter into the box. Close the lid.

~ Or, sing your favorite tune in your head. Say the words of the lyrics as if you are singing them out loud. Listen to the tune as it plays out in your mind.

Can you see how your mind has turned away from the reality around you and moved to a calmer place?

Some people can simply count numbers in their head, but this doesn't work for everyone. For some, it needs to be a more complex set of thoughts, enough to take their mind away from the stressful situation. All it takes is a few seconds of visualization. Of course, it doesn't take you away from whatever you are experiencing. It is a coping mechanism to calm your thoughts. Perhaps it will help you walk from a volatile situation the next time you feel your anger rising.

Understand Your Own Body

Often, uncontrolled negative emotions can be associated with traumas of some kind. The accumulation of many negative emotions can lead to depression and anxiety too. When this happens, it's not unusual for such individuals to feel negative about themselves. Negative life experiences do undoubtedly lead to low self- esteem.

The only person who can boost your confidence is you. You should have other people to help you, but it's you who has to alter the way you think. To do that successfully, you need to get to know yourself well. You need to understand who you have become and why you behave the way you do. Here are a few pointers to help you achieve such a notion.

Learn what your triggers are that lead to you to feeling insecure and make you lash out angrily? Do you:

- ❖ Lose your temper with everyone? Or do think you seem to home-in on one person in particular, such as your spouse or even your children?
- ❖ Feel like you can't stop yourself from lashing out, even to the point of hitting someone?
- ❖ Feel sick, sweaty, or breathless before you get to the final stage of aggression?
- ❖ Hate everyone? The world, people, politics?

Only by interrogating yourself can you understand the truth of your nature. There's no point lying to yourself. You need to know the raw truth of what's going on in your head.

Write things down, such as in a diary. It's not a diary of your everyday events; it's more so you can log down your emotions. Also note what you were doing at the time when you felt weepy, happy, or even angry. You can keep it private or share it with someone you trust for advice.

See if you can recognize a pattern in your behavior. Do you feel irritable after eating a particular food? You need to find out when and why you became irritated. Ask yourself these questions for as long as it takes to get to know yourself.

❖ Learn to alter your thought patterns.

If you don't agree with someone's opinions, hold back on telling them. When you do attempt to discuss the matter, try not to be too blunt. Perhaps you could ask them to explain what they mean a little better as it's a topic that you're interested in, even if you're not. Try to see their point of view as they explain. This is the start of practicing empathy, understanding other people's point of view on how they see a situation. Try to perceive how they feel rather than focusing on what you might be feeling. It's is a tall order, and it will be hard to do if your own personality is typically introvert.

If you can practice this, it's a way to try and see the world outside of your own head. You don't have to start liking people; it's more about listening and observing them. Make a start on those around you, most especially those in your close social network.

❖ Learn to listen to other people.

The next time someone is describing something that happened to them, listen without speaking. Instead of coming back at them with your own similar experience, hold back on your words. Don't share your own encounter; instead ask them questions about theirs. Show an interest in them. By doing this, you're forcing yourself to look outwards instead of inwards at yourself. This will also teach you to become more empathic towards others.

❖ Don't dwell on your bad experiences.

This could be one of the hardest of all to do. Someone who has anger issues and other psychological problems often only remembers the bad events in their lives. Bad experiences seem to dominate their memories and ultimately their lives.

We all seem to remember those awkward moments. Sometimes we can look back and laugh at them; others are too painful and still hurt our feelings. If you dwell on the negative, it can only lead to depression and anxiety.

If depression sets in, then other mental health issues are often not far behind. Yet, how can you fight away bad memories that have left you scarred?

It's a difficult path to explore, and you will need help to sort out the muddle in your mind. It could be that medication can help. Make an appointment with a doctor or clinician, so you get the right meds.

How does someone pick themselves up when they're at rock bottom?

There is no formal answer because each of us has different coping mechanisms.

- ~ Some people may lock bad memories away and never allow them out. This isn't a particularly good coping strategy. Relapses will be common and often at the least unexpected of times. Better to get them out and dealt with by asking for help from a professional.

- ~ Others may give in and turn to alcohol or recreational drugs to help them forget. This only serves to make their lives worse and their depression deeper.
- ~ If you want a "normal" lifestyle, whereby you can earn money for your family and protect them, then it's important to treat your emotions with respect. Seek help, and the professionals will show you many ways to cope until you find the right one that works for you.

To get your anger under control, you must take these first steps. Something is behind the reason why you feel the way you do. Admit that, and you can then seek to take steps to find help. Asking for help is never easy when your mind is not functioning clearly. To move on, though, you must swallow your pride and find help. With the right kind of guidance, you can make these changes gradually.

What though, can you do if you are the target of anger?

That's our next topic. It's never easy if the person you love is angry and abusive.

Chapter 9

Domestic Violence

When we fall in love, most of us don't consider the possible negative side of our new relationship.

More often than not, it is women who suffer the most, but men do suffer too.

Poverty and Familial Violence

- ❖ Up until the mid-1800s, husbands had a legal right to beat their wives. It was not until 1920 that "wife beating" finally became illegal in all states in the US.
- ❖ In 2011, the US CDC (Centers for Disease Control and Prevention) recorded 4.8 million abusive attacks reported by women and 2.9 million by men.
- ❖ Intimate Partner Violence (IPF) reports that 3 in 10 women and 1 in 10 men, suffer various forms of violence by partners.

❖ In 2007, IPF reported that of over two thousand deaths related to partner violence, 70% were women.

These are staggering statistics and spread out as a worldwide problem too. Globally, 1 in 3 women suffers violent attacks by their partner.

Domestic violence can and does happen in all walks of life. Studies are showing that the risks are greater within the poorer sectors of society. Those on lower incomes tend to suffer more stresses and strains of life. It is more difficult for this sector to maintain a decent living standard. Recent statistics show that up to 20% of children will witness some form of domestic violence. Unfortunately, this vicious circle continues on through generations of families. Good parenting skills will be low on the agenda for adults who have suffered abuse and income difficulties themselves. These are the children more likely to mature with behavioral problems. Low Income can be closely related to the development of mental health issues, though not always.

Such results paint a bleak picture of life for those on a low income. Indeed, violence within the family is the third leading reason for homelessness, according to the US Dept. of Housing. For many, anger issues are prevalent in the marital home.

We all like to feel that we're protected by the laws of our land, but that doesn't mean you can pass the buck. If you are the cause of hurting someone because you can't control your emotions, you owe it to your loved ones to repair the damage. That has to start with yourself. You must make changes to your inner self, and that will resonate outwards like the ripples in a pond. Of course, this can only work if you want it to. Sadly, there are plenty of angry people who have no intentions of changing and will never try. Again, I reiterate, you have to want to improve your lifestyle for those you love and for yourself.

If you are an angry person, learn to curb your temper and improve your lifestyle. A more positive outlook can be brought on with a better diet, exercise, and relaxation methods. Introducing these good habits into your life will put you on the path to success, not only for you but your family and friends too.

This is why guides such as this one might help to highlight that you CAN make changes. Take the time to learn about the underlying causes of anger so you can find solutions.

Causes of Anger in Relationships

With the first blush of romance, most relationships are rosy and sweet. The hormones take care of that as the brain gets flooded with certain chemicals, such as dopamine. Yes, once again, it's the chemicals in the brain that drive our emotions, even in love.

Biological changes affect our moods, and with romance, the hormones make us feel good. Once you experience that true deep affection, it can be hard to live without that person in your life. Over time though, things can change in any relationship, especially if one of the partners has an anger management issue.

Relationship Melt Down

❖ Scenario 1

At the start of a loving relationship, both partners may class themselves as "we." They are a couple and tend to do things together. If one partner starts thinking more in terms of "me," than "we," it can be difficult for the other partner to accept. Arguments may set in with differences of opinions. This can cause tempers to flare and the ultimate act of lashing out by one of the partners. When that happens, it can often mean the end of the relationship. For the one who is still in love, despite the anger and abuse, it can feel almost like grief. How do they live without a person who has been in their life so intimately? They seem to want to forget the aggression and return to what they once had.

❖ Scenario 2

Two young people fall in love and end up married with children. It seems the normal thing to do. As they go through each typical phase together, they become burdened with more and more responsibilities. Getting a home together seemed exciting at the beginning.

Once that home becomes a financial burden, all the fun disappears. Having a family was all they dreamed of. No one teaches us the burdens of becoming responsible for other people's lives.

Now the financial pressures are heavy. The young mothers often need to go out to work as well as manage the household. Couples spend less and less time together and begin to grow apart. As they do, it can involve an array of experiences, anything from having extramarital affairs to constant bickering.

In a relationship where romance has died, it can lead to making life-changing decisions. Often this can result in splitting up an entire family as divorce rears its ugly head.

It would be better if we could learn to recognize the early stages of a sour relationship, most especially if aggression becomes a factor. The last thing anyone wants is children witnessing their loving parents hurting each other. Nor will they want to take sides.

Signs of Stress

Stress can be a key factor in any relationship that is breaking down. The high emotional tension can easily lead to physical arguments. No one can foresee whether a sour relationship should battle on to see if they can get through and become happy again. Strong relationships still go through bouts of insecurity. If stress does set in, then you risk becoming ill. If you recognize such symptoms, then you must deal with healing yourself. If that involves separation for a while, then it's worth it before you become mentally ill.

- Tiredness
- Sleeping difficulties
- Unable to concentrate
- Making more and more mistakes
- Irritability
- Eating unhealthier foods for comfort
- Eating less as you have no appetite
- Having no time for yourself
- Not wanting to socialize
- Feeling ill, such as headaches, stomach aches, toilet problems, palpitations.

Acute stress from life's demands is exhausting. It's fine to experience short periods of stress; this is a part of living. If it goes hand in hand with an aggressive partner, then it can become more serious for your health. Chronic stress can make you short-tempered and hostile towards those you love. You may begin to smoke, or drink alcohol, or even take un-prescribed drugs to help you cope. If you never have time to do things that give you pleasure because all you want to do is get the day's routine over with so you can sleep, it's time to find out why. The trouble is that the stress doesn't go away if left untreated, and it may even turn into a deep depression. That's because you need to identify the root of the problem and tackle it.

There's no point if anyone tells you to snap out of it; the chances are you won't even realize you're stressed out. This is why it's important to recognize the symptoms we have discussed in this guide. If this sounds like you, then you need to take action.

Things can become even worse if you have an abusive partner or someone who is bullying you at work. Living with angry people only adds to a person's daily stresses. Resentment can turn into hatred. If you feel that the only time you have energy is when you both argue, it's the surge of adrenalin rushing through you. With that can also come an ability to behave recklessly. Such behavior could be something that might later be regretted.

How to Deal with an Angry Partner

Often anger that leads to violence is usually by a man who is the culprit. When it gets to the stage of violence, the man will be in no condition to listen or compromise as he puts fear into his partner. If you are the partner of such a person, here are a few immediate tips for the situation:

- ❖ Try to stay calm instead of lashing out with your own angry words. It might stop your partner from getting worse.
- ❖ Try to listen to the angry person's words and don't interrupt them. Let them have their say until they've finished. At that point, they are

completely immersed in their stress and are far more likely to lash out.

❖ Remain as positive as you can. If you can't say anything helpful, stay quiet. The last thing they need is someone acting hostile towards them. It may even trigger physical violence.

❖ Remember, there are two in an argument. If you can be the strong one and show compassion, you might be able to dampen their anger before it turns to violence.

If you are the victim of a violent relationship, you must assess your situation and make changes, particularly if you have children. Ask yourself:

Do you love your partner?

If so, can you convince them, when they are calmer, to seek help?

Violent people are insecure people. The quicker they become violent, the more insecure they are. They may not be comfortable with themselves. This means they'll have a terrible feeling of guilt and shame after their outbursts. The saying, "You always hurt the one you love," rings true in such cases. Most of us tend to feel annoyed at those we love the most when we get angry. In any relationship, though, it is going to take both parties to work together. Whether the angry person is your spouse, parent, child, or friend, here are a few tips to help them cope.

- ❖ The best time to reason with them over their behavior is when they are calm. That's the most likely time you will get through to them; they may even admit they know that they have a problem.
- ❖ Talk about how destructive and hurtful they can be when they lose all control. They need to know the raw truth to motivate them to stop their destructive behavior.
- ❖ Try to decipher if they feel depressed or suffer low self-esteem. If they do, then look at the options together on finding help.
- ❖ Assure them of your love and affection and ask them if you can go through it with them as you both find help together.

- ❖ Discuss the use of a "safe word" to let them know that you feel insecure about their behavior.
- ❖ Devise a regime together, such as how they can take time out for themselves. A good exercise regime can often help with discipline and anger control. A good diet will help too, as well as time to do things they enjoy.
- ❖ If the angry person in your life is already using alcohol or drugs, you must make the huge decision of whether you want that in your life. The added complication will delay them from being willing to get help. It can be done, though. Many an addict has pulled through because their loved ones helped them.
- ❖ If you are that person, then you seriously need to realize your problem. Again I repeat, addicts can and do pull through to turn their lives around. Coming off the alcohol or drugs will be no easy ride, but many of the addictive drugs may actually be the cause of the emotional moods. Once the body is rid of the poisons,

maybe a better future will be in sight and obtainable.

Problem-solving is about finding solutions, not about wading in pity. Every problem has a solution; you just need to find it. It may take years to resolve. But, if it means improving your lifestyle, it will be the best thing you can ever do for yourself and your loved ones.

Chapter 10

MANIPULATION AND ANGER

One major hurdle for those who feel irritable, annoyed, or angry for much of the time is that they are not willing to admit this. More often than not, they will be in denial. If you were to suggest as much to them, they would only become annoyed with you. Once they're left alone because they've pushed everyone away, perhaps then they may start to see that they have a problem. This is usually when it's too late, and much damage is done. Often with this type of personality, they feel that the problem is someone else's and not theirs. Angry people tend to block most of their emotions. All they are left with is the burning frustration of anger.

This can be even more difficult if they turn to alcohol or drugs to ease their troubled mind. Another factor at play may even be manipulation. If a person is manipulative, they force others to see to their needs and can even threaten them if they don't.

Narcissistic Personality Disorder (NPD)

These are people who want everyone to see them as good-natured. They will go to any lengths to become liked. Here is a guide of their typical characteristics so you can hopefully avoid them:

- Total lack of empathy
- Arrogant
- Self-centered
- Demanding
- Often talk with a loud voice
- Exploit others
- Seekers of admiration and like to be the center of attention
- Sensitive to criticism
- Always defensive
- Believe they are entitled to the best treatment for their own needs.

The main problem and there are many as you can see is that sometime a narcissist will often react with anger if things go wrong. They are highly controlling and may even view you as their property. Such possessiveness can lead to a horrendous type of jealousy on their part.

Devious Manipulation

- ❖ The manipulative, angry person can easily tap into another person's fears by discovering their weaknesses.
- ❖ Often, when you first meet such a character, they can come across as charming and generous to a fault. That's because they hide their aggressive nature at the beginning of a relationship. They will dig for your weaknesses and slowly take over your life.
- ❖ They may have no care if they hurt others because they lack the skill of empathy or even sympathy. Their world revolves around them and them only.

- ❖ Nothing is ever their fault, so they always blame others for everything that might go wrong in their daily lives.
- ❖ Often the victim of a manipulator is usually of a weaker character. Such people are more likely to have vulnerabilities.
- ❖ Everything they do is about their own gain and rewards.
- ❖ They have a great need to be in control as it gives them a feeling of power. They think of themselves as leaders.
- ❖ If they lose that control, they will most likely become angry and lash out.
- ❖ Such people don't care about social niceties; that's for everyone else, not them. Yet, they would be the first to complain if something happens that they don't like.
- ❖ These type of people are not good people to be around, and it will not be easy to get away from them if they do enter your life

Manipulation exists on many levels. Every time we see an advertisement, we are subtly manipulated by the sellers. These people, though, are not doing it for commercial gain, only for personal gain.

When an individual person tries to manipulate you, the chances are they are doing it for a sinister reason. They are selfish individuals who are out to control your life. Though they will never admit to it, they are suffering a personality disorder, and some are even extreme narcissistic, such as in the diagnosis of NPD.

Leaving a Manipulative Relationship

Do you live in a relationship with many flare-ups that make you feel afraid? It could be the reason you have made that all important decision of leaving. It is going to have its challenges, so you must be sure that is what you want. Your partner will try all sorts of tactics to stop you or get you back, and they will be painful for you to go through:

- ❖ They may change the entire situation around to make it look as though they are the victim, and you the perpetrator. One of their best tricks is to put you down as much as they can; it makes them feel powerful and in control.

❖ They will play on your emotions because they know your weaknesses.

❖ Gaslighting: It's when someone convinces you that you can't trust yourself. How they do this depends on the situation between you both. How they usually go about it is by causing you to feel confusion over time. Eventually, you will begin to question your own sanity.

❖ At first, you may get that dreaded silent treatment. Be thankful; their temper tantrums are much worse. Their pettiness will hold no boundaries as they try to make you feel guilty.

❖ You will need to plan your departure ahead of time, and if possible, find someone you can trust so they can help you, particularly if you are taking children with you. If your partner has made sure you don't have any friends left, then look up some help lines. At the very least you need someone, even a stranger, to talk through your escape plan because that is what it is.

❖ Organize somewhere to stay before you leave, even if it's only temporary.
❖ If your partner is prone to violence, then leave when they're not around. You could leave a note, so they know exactly what has happened. Or, leave nothing to give yourself some time to get ahead of the game.
❖ Ideally, you want to be a good distance away from them when they find out. They are going to try to get you back, using dirty tactics such as:
  ~ Behaving over-emotional and repentant, even to the point of breaking down to cry in front of you. It will be very dramatic in nature.
  ~ They may even threaten to commit suicide if you don't go back to them. It's a difficult situation to be in, but you must push ahead and ignore their threats.
  ~ When the anger comes, and it will, they will blame you. No doubt they will spread rumors and may even tell lies about you. Be prepared for the worse.

- ❖ You need to change all your contact information, such as replacing your sim card, so they don't know your new number. Keep your address a secret to start with, though they could come to your place of work and embarrass you. They may also try the sweet talk with flowers and gifts. It's all a show; try not to be taken in! If they insist they will change, remember you are walking on eggshells. The only chance of them changing is if they seek professional help. Should they agree to that, you would be best to remain separate for a few months to see if it happens.

Some manipulators are not as bad as others. If your partner rules your life and is violent with it, they are the worse kind. This may be the type of partner whereby you need to go to the police for a restraining order, so they leave you alone. Such dominating partners can turn into stalkers because they become obsessed with a person in their life.

It can be a difficult time for those who are the victim of a manipulative and violent person. If you feel threatened, then you must leave immediately, ideally when they're not around. You will most likely lose most of your possessions. Your safety and the safety of your children is paramount. Any loss is insignificant when compared to the possible violent repercussions. They may see you as a betrayer and look to seek revenge. You are going to need all the help you can get, so don't be afraid to ask. If you manage to get the perpetrator out of your life, you will become so much happier.

Chapter 11

THE IMPORTANCE OF EMPATHY

Whilst empathy is not something an angry person is likely to have, it is something that we should all strive to improve upon. If we all worked at becoming more empathic, the world would indeed be a better place.

Some people have so little empathy for others and the world around them that they don't even know what it is. Let's lay it out so that if they happen upon this guide, they have no excuse.

What is Empathy?

First, let's make it clear what it is not. Empathy is not the same as sympathy.

When you have sympathy for someone's situation, you most likely feel sorry for them. You might even pity them.

When you empathize for someone's situation, you feel the pain they are going through. You should be able to put yourself in their situation to understand their emotions. It's not about feeling sorry for them or pitying them. If you can feel their desperation, then you will also have a longing to alleviate their troubles.

What then has the empathy to do with anger? It is a form of therapy that could completely change your life around, should you suffer bitter, angry moments on a regular basis.

Empathic Anger Management (EAM)

This type of therapy does not replace your relaxation routine, such as breathing and visualizing exercises. It complements such techniques.

Aggressively angry people are ego-centric, as they believe that everything revolves around them. This can often result from a lack of support for their inner emotions. With no help for their bitter emotions, it means they have managed their emotions the best they could, their only supporter being themselves. In this situation, where unsupported self-help was the only option, it is like "The blind leading the blind." Someone who is already deep in negative thoughts cannot help themselves to climb out of such dark places. Instead, they spiral deeper within their negative outlook. After all, they can only see the world from their own perspective.

Sometimes we are so knee-deep in our own-self, that we become the center of that little world. By learning compassion and empathy, that inner world will open up. They will come to realize that there are many, many others who suffer too and some even worse than themselves.

It doesn't work for everyone, particularly for those with manipulative anger. This type of therapy will only work with someone who has a desire to overcome and control their regular angry outbursts.

Relationships

Any good relationship needs empathy, sacrifice, forgiveness, and learning to be non-judgmental.

For example, let's consider the relationship in a long-term marriage. It's unlikely that any extended relationship does not involve arguments in some form or other from time to time. Those who have been together for many years will confirm that it is:

- ❖ The art of compromising that glues their relationship together.
- ❖ The skill to understand what the other partner's needs are, even if they clash with their own.
- ❖ Making sacrifices, so others also find some happiness.
- ❖ About not putting other people down because they aren't the same as yourself.

These are caring characteristics that will seem alien to an aggressively angry person. Without empathy, compassion, and sacrifice from both partners, a relationship will become very one-sided. That's how the aggressively angry person will have lived their entire lives. They don't know how to balance a friendship.

The absence of knowing how to think about another person has left them with a rather selfish personality. The next chapter covers this topic in more depth because these are the fundamental characteristics of becoming a GOOD person.

Cooling Routine

The next time you feel your anger building up:

- ❖ Take those deep breaths we mentioned earlier.
- ❖ Listen to your thoughts before saying another word.
- ❖ Question yourself as to why you feel this way
    - ~ "Why do I think it's their fault?"
    - ~ "What have they done to make me feel that way?"
    - ~ "Even it is their fault, does it really matter?"
- ❖ Ask yourself, why they might have acted the way they have. Try to see the situation from the other person's point of view.

This set of questions won't work in all situations. It's merely a guide to show you how to think before you react? Stop for a moment before you lash out with anger and listen to the voice in your head. By forcing yourself to question your actions, you are immediately putting a brake on any aggression.

The best part of questioning your thoughts in this way is that you are coercing yourself to look at the argument from a different point of view than your own. You are working towards empathy, though you're not quite there yet. It does take time to learn this skill if you don't feel it in a natural way.

When you do speak, your emotions should be calmer. Try to make your words empathic, by asking them questions about why they feel as they do, or what they mean by their word? Don't ask in a sarcastic voice; you need to sound genuine.

To diffuse an anger outburst, all you need to do is take a little time to try to understand both points of view. This is not an easy task when in the middle of a row. Everyone wants to shout out their own version of the story. If this is happening, stop yourself from responding other than to listen.

- ❖ Take that deep breath.
- ❖ Think with compassion.
- ❖ Ask yourself questions
- ❖ Ask the other person questions and listen to their answers. Even if you don't like what they're saying, try not to speak. Instead, shift your mind to understand why they feel the way they do. This is where the non-judgmental part is useful.
- ❖ Wait until they have finished speaking before you reply.

Do this, and you will reduce the intensity of the situation. You might even have a quieter conversation as you listen to one another.

You've learned how to listen, but there's more to do yet. The next stage is a little harder because it is about learning to make sacrifices.

- Sometimes, no matter how right you think you are, it might be better for everyone, including yourself, if you simply give in. That is the first step in making sacrifices. Though it might feel as if it goes against the grain of how you normally react when you feel angry. Yet, it should put a stop to the argument and ensure it doesn't escalate.

If you still feel infuriated inside, then you must force yourself to walk away from the situation. Continue to ask yourself questions instead of shouting in your head that it's all someone else's fault. Your internal anger needs to vent, go for a run, or just keep walking. Exercise is a great way to calm yourself down.

You must practice to keep this up whenever you think you are going to boil over with anger. You don't have to like what others are saying, but you do have to try to see their point of view.

Here's a situation on how an angry person can use empathy in a petty argument before he boils up with an aggressive response.

Case Scenario:

You're in the middle of a heated argument with your partner over the TV.

Take that breath through your nose, hold it, and let your stomach inflate. Let it go through your mouth.

Instead of using a loud voice to respond angrily to your partner, ask yourself if you understand exactly what the problem is. If you don't, then ask your partner calmly, "Explain why you're so upset with me?"

It could be that you're always in control of the remote and they're fed up with it. Whatever reason they give you now's the time to put yourself in their shoes. Would you like to live with someone who always chose what to watch on the TV? Would you like to be forced to always have to watch someone else's TV programs? I know this seems a trivial problem, but often the fiercest of arguments start from the smallest of problems.

This is the vital part, putting yourself in their situation to see if you could cope with it.

Next, you're going to have to make that sacrifice of admitting that you were wrong and work out how to share the TV.

By learning to become more understanding of others, you are substituting your anger for tolerance. That will make a huge difference in your life and for your loved ones too.

Chapter 12

THERE IS A GOOD SIDE TO ANGER

We've seen how anger is mostly considered a negative emotion. Yet anger is as natural as any other emotion, such as feeling happy or sad. Anger is not always an emotion to feel ashamed of. Sometimes, it is necessary to go through it so you can move on with your life. This is when anger can be positive. Anger can have a purpose in our lives.

Turn Your Anger Into a Useful Tool

❖ Boost of Confidence

If we want something really hard and can't get it, the frustration can cause us to feel angry. That doesn't mean it's bad to feel angry. It's an emotion that motivates us to try harder to achieve the object of our desires. Used in this way, so long as we're not acting with aggression, it's quite a useful tool to have. It means that we have set aside our inhibitions. That's because our thoughts are so focused on the injustice of not having what we need. This increases our confidence to allow us to negotiate better for ourselves. The anger stops us from feeling intimidated, so we're less likely to back down.

- ❖ Optimism

Research has shown a correlation between anger and optimism. One study was based on the differences of optimism in the genders. When confronted with the threat of a terrorist attack, 80% of the group felt angry, and they were men. However, they were more optimistic about possible future attacks believing they were less likely to happen. The other 20% of the group were women, and their reactions were different. They were more likely to feel fear instead of anger. They were also more pessimistic and worried about further attacks. Women believed if one attack had happened, then others could soon follow. The women had a more pessimistic risk assessment than men in this study.

❖ Protection

When we experience anger, it means that we are ready to protect ourselves. This can be useful in a relationship as it helps us express our feelings when someone has hurt us. Once again, we let down our guard and voice our opinions because we are experiencing anger. It's as if it gives us a protective shield making us stronger and more capable of defending ourselves.

❖ Anger in Grief

A time in our lives when we may be prone to a strange sort of anger is if we are unfortunate enough to suffer the loss of a loved one. Many mixed emotions will leave us in turmoil, and this can often turn to anger at the person you have lost. It's a time when we are emotionally distraught and will go through various stages of confusion. People deal with grief in different ways. It's important not to deny yourself the grieving process because it's essential to be able to move on. Without it, you may even feel angry with everyone around you. How can they all get on with their lives as if nothing has happened?

While you show your anger, you are physically connecting with other people, and that's a good thing. If you're not normally an aggressive person, then don't worry. It's unlikely that your anger will go anything beyond a snappy response. You need to feel this type of anger as it will lead to the next stage of the grieving process. Every stage plays its part so you can come out the other side with the acceptance of your loss.

❖ Self-Assessment

Often, when we have an angry episode, we can surprise ourselves by how domineering we can become. Afterward, as we calm down, it's not unusual to replay the scene out in our minds. Only then do we take notice of our own behavior and wonder if we went too far. This process causes us to self-assess our own behavior. We may reprimand ourselves for taking out our anger on other people. It's a form of self-improvement as you assess your own performance and seek to improve your own behavior.

❖ Avert Aggression

When people become angry and loud, it can be a signal to themselves and to others that the situation is becoming untenable. Sometimes, in the right situation, this can be a trigger for others to offer help to calm down the situation. It can act as a buffer from potential violence before an aggressive episode happens, so it serves as a warning. If you recall, we mentioned earlier in this guide that anger is not violence. It is an emotion, whilst violence is an action. In many cases when the noise of anger is heard, it's a chance for someone to help mediate the rising emotions. Sadly, this is not always the case as most of us only want to go in the opposite direction. For the trained ears and eyes though, it is an opportunity to intervene. If the perpetrators are not normally of an aggressive disposition, such intervention can prove useful.

❖ Righteous

This is a force that seeks justice where wrongdoings occur. In its raw form, anger allows us to seek justice by expressing our opinion. Under normal circumstances, we might not do this, so our anger edges us on. With this powerful force of strength, we protect ourselves to make sure no one takes advantage of us. It gives us a sense of boosted confidence.

- ❖ Therapeutic

Believe it or not, anger can be very therapeutic. That's because it helps us to discharge or vent our negative emotions. You might share angry words with a friend on how your neighbor played loud music all night long. By the time you've finished telling the tale, the chances are you feel much better. You are now unlikely to go and confront your neighbor with those same angry thoughts. Sharing your frustrations with a friend or loved one means you can vent without causing any harm. This releases your negative emotions in a safe setting. Anger can be constructive when controlled. If not controlled, then it can turn into rage.

By viewing anger as a normal healthy emotion, you won't feel the need to hide it. Don't deny yourself this natural emotion because it does have beneficial properties. Anger is an evolutionary adaptation that has its place inside your thoughts. It's not an emotion to fear. If you can control it, you can use it for the reasons outlined in this chapter. It's merely a means to express ourselves, so in a sense, it's a communication tool.

No one particularly likes conflict but it is a way of ensuring fairness where there is an injustice. Sharing anger is the best way to control such a situation. It allows us to inform others so they see our point of view on a situation. It helps us to get the "other side of a story" across. You might not have even seen that point of view had it not been for your own outburst. Being open and honest, as most of us are when in the anger-zone, it can help to prevent grudges from building up. When controlled, it can clear the air of any potential storm.

Ancient Chinese methods believed that each of the body organs represents an emotion. For anger, it is the liver and gallbladder. They concluded that if you can control your anger, these organs will function well. Whereas out of control anger will lead to digestive distresses as these organs suffer. Sounds pretty close to the truth!

Make your anger work for you by controlling it and utilizing its effects. By all means, use it to get the things that you want out of life. At the same time, don't abuse it or let it run out of control. Make good use of it by helping victims of injustices. That way, it becomes the tool of protection, which is what it should be. There's no denying that anger can cloud your judgment. That's all the more reason to keep it under control and make it work for you and not against you.

Chapter 13

BECOMING A GOOD PERSON

Changes on the Horizon

We've already looked at empathy, sacrifice, forgiveness, and learning to be non-judgmental.

Can you change your personality to include more of these positive characteristics?

Of course, you can, but there may be something that is stopping you. The wall of resistance could be your anger issues.

There is good news, though. If you can learn to understand the true concept of these characteristics, you're one step closer to making your anger issues disappear.

So, what exactly is a good person? Indeed, do any even exist on the planet earth?

Let's clear up the concept of a good person before we answer these questions. Everyone experiences anger because it is a human emotion. Chapter 12 showed us how anger does not have to be a bad experience. We can utilize this explosive emotion to improve our lives. A good person still experiences anger. What gives them the label of being "Good," is that they don't take their anger out on other people. A "good" person is a "caring" person. They can't possibly care about everyone in the world, though they probably do their best to care for nature too. They will practice all the good characteristics we have mentioned earlier in this chapter

By implying there are good people means that there must also be bad people. Sadly, this is raw the truth of our world, but that bad person does not have to be you. Even if you suffer violent outbursts, it does not mean that you are bad. If you know that you have hurt other people both emotionally and physically, then you are admitting your faults. You can still change. It can't happen overnight. As with any new skill, you must allow yourself a period of training.

Books such as this one are a great start in turning your life around.

Forgiveness

You already know the qualities of empathy. So, let's begin this guidance section on forgiveness.

Forgiveness is a major factor in being able to forgive others when you feel they have done you wrong. It's only when you can view a situation from another person's point of view as in empathy, that you can learn to forgive.

- ❖ It's crucial that you switch the focus from yourself, using those empathic skills. This is the only way to review a situation from someone else's point of view.
- ❖ It's also about learning to let go. Even if someone has done you an injustice, ask yourself, "Does it really matter?"

Of course, there are experiences in life that we simply cannot forgive. This is particularly so if we were children at the time or if it involves our loved ones. As we become adults, if something bad happened in our past, we find it difficult to let go. When we recall the bad memories, we are viewing them with our inner child's mind. It's not until we reach the ending of our teenage years that we can start to take control of our lives. Up until then, we rely on other adults to guide us. Some of us draw the short straw on the parents we end up with. In such cases, we don't have very good role models.

If you suffer recurring memories of bad experiences, you must consider some kind of therapy. Once you become an adult, you have the power to let go and move on. If you can't find that power, then get some help to overcome your problematic obstacles. The bad memories will never go away completely, but they'll become less important as an adult.

Forgiving the people who do you harm in your life is a difficult challenge. It is not the people in your past that matter any longer; it's those who you have in your present. Bad memories can make you an unhappy adult, but now you have the power to make your own decisions. Learn ways to cope with the past so you can move on to the future with a more positive outlook on life.

If you can achieve this, you can overcome your negative emotions and become a stronger person, the type of person who can learn to forgive others instead of resenting everyone who annoys you in some way. Some people will always try taking advantage of others. Instead of feeling angry with them, help them to understand what they did wrong. Allow yourself to forgive their transgressions and either walk away or help them.

Sacrifice

For example, imagine you are in a heated argument. You can see the other person is genuinely upset, but you can't stop yourself. You're becoming agitated because you know that your side of the story is the truth of the matter. Your anger is beginning to grow at their inability to see your side of the story. What do you do? The angry side of you wants to fight to the bitter end to get your point over. The empathic side of you will concede the argument to the other party. If you can do this, you have learned to sacrifice. Your mind stayed open to accept that it did not matter who was right and who was wrong. All that mattered was ending the upset cause by arguing. The result will allow the tension to dissipate.

As you learn such skills as sacrifice, you're also learning how to compromise. Compromising isn't about being right; it's about being sensible. To compromise is often to sacrifice because you will not be getting your own way. For an aggressively angry person, this would never be acceptable. They could not cope with other people winning them over. Yet, this is what you need to sacrifice for the sake of your health and the health of your loved ones.

If you are that person who explodes at every turn in your life, you can learn to sacrifice and compromise. Do this, and you can finally turn over a new leaf. There is much personal satisfaction in allowing other people to win the day. Even when you still believe that your point of view was the right one. Do this, and it means you have learned to sacrifice at the cost of your own feelings.

Being Non-judgmental

This may be the hardest skill of all for an aggressively angry person to overcome. Such people love to put everyone into boxes and categories. It gives them a sense of order in their inner turmoil. Their view of balance, though, is at the cost of judging others how they see them. Making up their own rules of how things should be. It's a form of personal labeling based on their own unbalanced judgment.

By being judgmental, we are assuming the outcome of everything should be the same.

For example, your neighbor gets arrested for shouting at his partner and disturbing the peace. You tell everyone that he deserved it because he's poor, fat, gay, black, or white. Yet, what gives you the right to come to that conclusion? You have judged the neighbor on gender, color, body build, or even on income. The truth is that the neighbor was arrested for none of those reasons. By assuming they were arrested for anything other than disturbing the peace, which was the truth, you are being judgmental. If you don't know the truth of a situation, then don't make assumptions.

For someone who is aggressive in nature, they will always believe that their version is the true one, even at the cost of incorrectly labeling a person by their own conceived and ill-judged opinions.

A good person would approach the partner left behind and help them with the situation. Clearly, our example family were already suffering difficulties. These will now have grown tenfold with one being arrested. They don't need labeling; what they need is help. If they don't want your help, then at last you tried. That is what you should aim to do with your life; try to help others with kindness and not with blame.

Chapter 14

MAINTAINING EQUILIBRIUM IN YOUR LIFE

Balance is the key factor when trying to attain a life of contentment.

There's no denying that the world can be a cruel place to live in. Some people can stagger from one bad experience to another, often with deadly consequences. It could be freak weather, a traumatic accident, or the death of a loved one, none of which we have any control over.

On the other side of the coin, we can also experience many amazing events such as the birth of a child, the love of a pet, finding a soul mate, or simply watching the sunset in a fiery, red sky over the ocean.

Given that we are bound to come across events we can't control, it makes sense to include as many positive ones as we can. That means avoiding bad experiences that we DO have control over.

If you're trying hard to control your anger but have a relapse, then it's not an excuse to let everything go. It may take a lifetime to turn things around and keep them that way. When things don't go the way you want them to, it's good to use the experience as a learning curve. You must learn that when you fail, the only option open to is to pick yourself up again and get back on track.

There will be days when you feel you can't keep battling your own personality just for the sake of those around you. Consider your transition like a dance, three steps forward, one step back. If you find you're unable to control yourself, at least turn away from the problem and scream up at the sky if you must. Do anything to stop yourself from confronting another person, whether you feel they deserve it or not.

Even calming down your own negative emotions doesn't mean that others will stop showing their anger towards you. Should such an episode happen, it may have the potential to unbalance you. This will be a provoking moment and one you may not be able to control. Think through how good it will make you feel if you can walk away.

Responding is the easy option; walking away takes courage.

Alternative Responding Mechanisms.

One of the best things you can teach yourself is that even when someone is in the wrong, it doesn't matter. The world will not end if you concede their point. Teach yourself what is really important in your life.

Here are some annoying situations with alternative responses:

Situation 1:

If someone insults you or one of your loved ones.

Past Response

You would respond with aggression.

New Response

At the end of the day, their insult is only their personal opinion. If this person is not anyone important to you, why does it matter what they think? You have to learn to pull away from an aggressive situation.

Situation 2:

Your partner has left all the dirty pots and gone to bed. It looks like they expect you to do them.

Past Response

You would confront them aggressively, asking them with sarcasm in your tone if they thought an invisible fairy was going to do the dishes.

New Response

Why not do the dishes and say nothing at that point? When you have some time, create a roster of certain housework tasks. Present it to them with a genuine smile and not in an aggressive way. Explain that it might lighten the load to share things equally.

Situation 3:

A driver overtook you when there was no need because you're driving at the right speed limit.

Past Response

This would infuriate you. You'd start swearing and shouting in the car, or even open the window to do it, regardless of passengers.

New Response

STOP allowing things that other people do to annoy you so much. Yes, they were wrong, but there's nothing you can do about it once it's happened. If you get annoyed, you are running the risk of increasing your blood pressure as well as upsetting your passengers. Ask yourself, is it worth it?

Sure, it's so much easier to say what the outcome of a dispute should be when you're not in it, but that's the whole point. You have to learn to distance yourself from situations that cause your emotions to boil up. Pull your thoughts away from your negative responses. At worst, ignore the situation or walk away from it. At best, do your relaxation breathing and handle the situation with a more positive outlook.

Don't be a quitter!

Here are a few situations that might cause you to relapse:

❖ It's very hard to change a characteristic you've had all your life.

There's no denying that this is going to be difficult. Stopping a behavior that happens automatically without any real thought is a challenge in itself. That's why it's important to have a network of support. Although you are the only person who can force the changes, you don't have to do it alone.

This process of change should be done in stages. No one expects you to change on day one. Find a way of rewarding yourself every time you manage to control those anger outbursts. Don't forget that your reward is also in seeing those around much happier. They will love you all the more now that you're not losing your temper all the time.

- ❖ "They were getting on my nerves."

Concentrate more on your empathic skills when this happens.

Ask yourself why they are doing what they're doing. Search for the reasons and don't give up until you've calmed down.

Walk away, so you don't have to face-up to whoever is offending you. It's far better to walk away than start an argument that can only end up unbalancing your emotions.

- ❖ "It was their fault!"

Ask yourself, does it really matter who's fault it is?

What will that achieve?

It cannot undo any harm that's already happened.

Don't look for blame. Instead, look for solutions.

It has taken you a lifetime to be the person you are. Whatever life events you have lived through, they have made you into who you are. That's a lifetime of rich experiences. Take that knowledge and use it to strengthen your positive side so you can become a person who is content with their lot. Learn to push away angry thoughts. Write them down when they happen and use the notes to understand when and why you felt that way. Decide on a way forward to overcome your negative thinking patterns. Such thoughts and memories can only hold you back.

Chapter 15

Natural Healing

Natural remedies often complement prescribed medication. If you decide to try natural healing, you must research and check there are no clashes with any prescribed medication, although it's unlikely. If you're unsure, then consult your physician

There are various natural ways to help your psychological wellbeing, including:

- ❖ Deep breathing routine.
- ❖ Visualization.
- ❖ Peaceful walking with nature around you like in woodland or on a beach.
- ❖ Muscle flexing and relaxing throughout your body.
- ❖ Swimming and cycling.
- ❖ A healthy diet.
- ❖ A good night's sleep.

If you're considering cycling as a means for mental wellbeing, then avoid busy roads. That will not relax your mind. It's about finding ways to relax your mind and body as soon as you feel your anger or stress taking hold. If one thing worked for all, it would be wonderful, but it's not that easy. We all know that different things work for different people.

Also, consider natural herbal remedies. Whilst they may not be scientifically backed, many have been around for hundreds if not thousands of years. These are plant-based oils, seeds, and paste. Each has different properties to help with varying conditions. There are plenty of herbs that ease stress, anxiety, and depression. Here are a few that can be bought over the counter often as capsules, oils, teas, and seeds.

- ❖ St John's Wort has properties that help with mood swings.
- ❖ Valerian is helpful for a relaxing sleep, but you should not take it with any other sleeping medication.
- ❖ Passionflower also has a sedative effect, helping with both relaxation and sleep.

- ❖ Chamomile makes a great tea that you should consider using regularly. If you don't like the taste on its own, add some honey or lemon to it.
- ❖ Lavender's aroma is delightful. Studies have shown that inhaling its scent can help relax your mind.
- ❖ Lemon balm and mint all make for a lovely scent in your home. Mint tea will help with stomach problems, so will ginger tea.

If you don't want to consume these natural remedies, consider buying the oils to burn around your home. Essential oils are the best as they have little in the way of additives, so you're in safe hands when smelling these natural aromas.

If you're pregnant or take prescribed medication, you should check with your doctor that it is safe to use your chosen herbal remedies.

Here are a few more to add to your list of research to find the right one for you.

- ❖ Ginseng is great for giving you an added boost of energy.
- ❖ Garlic lowers your cholesterol levels, so get using it in your healthy cooking.
- ❖ Green teas will help your digestive system.
- ❖ Milk thistle is good for your liver, helping to repair damaged cells.
- ❖ Bilberries help with blood circulation. There is also evidence they can help with diabetes and cholesterol levels. Cranberry juice is good if you have a urine infection.

It can take a few weeks before you see any positive effects from herbal remedies. Start with a low dosage to make sure you don't have a negative reaction. There are many brands available, and it can be difficult to decide which products to buy. As a guide, you should look for the product with the highest active ingredients. Any quality product should also have an expiry date. Do follow the instructions, especially if you're taking other medication.

There are some plant-based foods that people can enjoy, but they can do us more harm than good.

- ❖ Coffee contains the caffeine that we crave if we need an energy boost. It's meant to help with concentration. The trouble is there are side effects if you use too much. You may become irritable or feel palpitations. If you have it late in the day, you might also suffer insomnia too. Too much caffeine is not good for your digestive system either. You can do without these problems when you're under stress. Try not to have more than around 100 grams of coffee on a daily basis. This means you can still enjoy the taste and benefits without it harming your health.
- ❖ Chocolate has also been in the media quite a lot lately. There are properties in it that can help to reduce stress levels and have a calming effect. If you are a chocolate lover, this does not mean that you can eat large amounts. To benefit from the cocoa bean, you should buy dark chocolate that has at least 70% cocoa content. For

instance, 100 grams will contain around 600 calories that also include sugars and fats. Look for bars of chocolate where coco is high on the ingredients list, and sugar is further down. If you see the words "alkali" or "ditching" on the label, don't buy it. It is a form of processing that changes the color and also reduces the beneficial effects.

❖ Red wine is another product that causes confusion. Whilst it is true that dry red wines contain some natural anti-inflammatory properties, it's not true that you can drink lots of it. All alcohol should be consumed in moderation. There's no reason why you can't enjoy the odd a 5 oz. glass of dry red wine a few times a week. This isn't a large glass, but it will be a nice treat with a few pieces of that dark chocolate.

Conclusion

Who would have thought that controlling anger could be so complex? Then again, humans are a convoluted lot. When it comes to human emotions, you must have realistic expectations. Nothing is going to happen overnight!

Our emotions form an intricate web of who we are as individuals. How we react to situations is dependent on what we have experienced throughout our own lives. Such experiences have helped to form our own personality. We must respect an individual's faults as well as their good side because it's taken them a lifetime to get there.

This book shows how anger can be managed. The perpetrator must be a willing participant, ready and willing to strive for a new lifestyle and outlook. It's not only for loved ones and friends that their anger needs to be controlled but also for their own wellbeing. The constant release of certain hormones that happens when a person is angry will have a long-term negative effect on their health. It can do no good to be continuously on alert, which is what they are, with anger.

We can become so wrapped up in our own negative thoughts that we are unable to see the world around us. It's not necessarily about being one with nature, but the outside world has much to offer. Many men love to go fishing and stand for hours on a peaceful, grassy embankment. They may not admit it, but they have found peace with nature. There are various aspects that will help anyone suffering from negative thoughts. If this is you, we will discuss how you can find a mindset of positive thinking. Only then can you appreciate the world and people around you.

Depression is a terrible, lonely condition. Those who have anger issues tend to suffer from low self-esteem, depression, and relationship issues. No one wants to be alone because we are social creatures at heart. Nor do we always want people in our face, but we do need some form of contact with our fellow human beings. It's vital not to see other people as your enemy. We all have their own demons to face, so we need to give each other space.

The advice in this book will not work for everyone. There are those who are happy being downright aggressive and manipulating. The rest of us should avoid such people. Often it can be that they have suffered irreparable damage and are unlikely to admit that they need help.

The key point of this book is that you MUST WANT to change. That is the main motivation and driving force to improving your lifestyle. None of us is the perfect human being; we all have flaws. It's when those defects involve hurting other people that you must open your eyes and admit that what you are doing is wrong. Inflicting pain on others, whether mental or physical, is the most selfish act a human can do. We have the intelligence to know better, and I'm not talking about academic intelligence.

Put your personal grievances aside and push on to overcome your negative thinking. There will always be someone who will annoy you out there. If you can become a better person inside your own mind, you won't even notice them. That's because you will learn to rise above the small things in life that have unbalanced you in the past. If you can turn your aggression into love, it will not be a miracle that has happened. It will be your own hard work to overcome those mental health issues that have dragged you down for such a long time.

Those of you who follow the advice in this guide and then implement the changes are set to become better people.

COGNITIVE BEHAVIORAL THERAPY

By

DANIEL SHEPHERD
TOM WALLACES

INTRODUCTION

I want to thank you for choosing this book, 'Cognitive Behavioral Therapy: The Key Lessons for Beginners on How CBT is used in Retraining the Brain to Overcome Depression, Anxiety and Negative Thinking Using Practical Techniques and Hypnosis' and hope that it helps you understand Cognitive Behavioral Therapy or CBT as it is commonly called.

You probably go in for a regular health check-up every six months or at least once a year. Every time you fall sick or hurt yourself, you probably consult a doctor. But these are all physical injuries and most people only pay heed to these. Somehow, being able to see a cut or bruise makes it a valid illness, but something we can't see or understand is ignored.

At some point or the other, everyone has negative feelings, depression, or stress. Did you ever consult someone to deal with it? Usually, people just like to work through it by them and are somehow ashamed of admitting they need help. You need to understand that physical injuries need care, but a little medicine and some bandages will heal them up quickly. Mental health, however, is just as important but more complicated to deal with. Feeling sad about something for a while is completely different from suffering from depression, mental trauma, and just illnesses. There is never any shame in admitting that your mind needs some healing and that you need to reach out for help.

Mental issues can be much more complex than you realize and need professional help. Over the past couple of years, mental health has been gaining a lot more attention as people realize that it is just as crucial as physical health. When was the last time you looked for treatment for mental issues that are affecting your daily life and mental stability? You do not have to compare your problems with others and feel like yours are not big enough to deserve attention. Everyone has his or her own issues, and each one is equally valid and deserves to be addressed.

One of the treatments that are used for dealing with mental health issues like depression, personality disorders, stress, etc. is Cognitive Behavioral Therapy. This book will help you understand what this therapy is and how it can help in mental health treatment. If you are reading this book, you have taken the first step to admitting that you need help. Learning about Cognitive Behavioral Therapy will help you understand the methods involved in it and will help you utilize it to restore peace to your mind. This therapy has involved a lot of study and research and is used to treat anxiety, depression, addictions, stress, and such issues that can seriously affect your mental health and daily life.

Mental illness is just as common and important as physical illness. If you leave it untreated for too long, it can build up and seriously affect your daily life. Physical illness just affects your body, and at most it will leave a scar once you treat it. Mental illness will affect you and the people around you. Leaving such issues unaddressed will have a negative impact on yourself and your relationships with other people as well as your work life. All the information in this book is meant to help you in improving the quality of your thoughts and your quality of life. There are many reasons why people get stuck in bad situations, and negative thoughts are one of the main reasons for this.

Changing your mindset and dealing with mental issues will help you to turn things around for the better. You have to recognize negative behavior and thoughts and change them to achieve better things in your life. So, take a step and start the journey to gain peace in your life again.

Thank you once again for choosing this book. I hope you find it informative. the only thing I ask is if you could please leave an honest review after listening.

Chapter 1

YOUR THOUGHT PROCESS

Your thought process is how your mind works or thinks about something. Everyone has a unique mind and thus a unique way of thinking and processing things. The brain is one organ on which there is always extensive research being conducted, and yet there is never any definitive understanding of it. Each individual has a thought process by which they use their mind to carefully consider something.

Thinking and reasoning are cognitive abilities that distinguish humans from other species. Everything a person faces in life is dealt with using reasoning and their thinking capacity. The power of this process is an essential tool in survival. Thinking and reasoning are essential for everyone to lead a good life.

Types of thinking

If you want to classify thinking into types, they would be as follows:

Perceptual thinking

Perceptual thinking is the simpler form of thinking and is based on a person's perception. This means that it is how a person interprets sensations from a particular experience. This type of thinking is called concrete thinking because it is based on the perception of concrete things.

Conceptual thinking

Also known as abstract thinking, conceptual thinking allows a person to make use of generalized concepts. It is considered superior to concrete thinking because it involves some effort in solving problems and understanding things.

Reflective thinking

Reflective thinking is the type that tries to solve complex problems. This is done by reorganizing relevant experiences concerning a situation and also by removing obstacles. The mental activity in reflective thinking does not involve trial and error efforts, so it is a more insightful approach. Reflective thinking involves rearrangement of relevant facts to reach a logical conclusion and find a solution.

Creative thinking

Creative thinking is linked with the person's ability to create a novel or new thing. It describes and interprets the nature of modern relationships. The person uses evidence and tools to find a solution. Creative thinking comes in all shapes and forms and is an entirely internal process. It is an integral part of cognitive behavior. Every person is capable of creative thinking. This type of thinking allows something new to be formed every time. Unlike convergent thinking, creative thinking involves different dimensions of thought. It covers many aspects of an individual's life and is very comprehensive.

Critical thinking

Critical thinking helps a person to step aside from their prejudices, personal beliefs or opinions and assess the truth. It is done even at the expense of disregarding a person's own belief system. This type of thinking involves higher cognitive ability and skill, and this helps in interpreting, analyzing and evaluating a situation. It helps the person to reach an inference from the unbiased gathered judgment. Critical thinking can be a self-regulatory mechanism that can be beneficial to the person. The person must have an open mind and be fair in his judgment. He cannot use bias and personal prejudices to decide on something. Their skills of interpretation, analysis, evaluation, etc. all have to be up to the mark. Critical thinking is a more complex and higher way of thinking. It utilizes cognitive skills to reach a reliable and valid judgment from the gathered information.

Non-directed thinking

Sometimes your thinking can go off in an undirected way and has no goal. It can be a unique type of thought process that is reflected in the form of dreams and random activities. This type of thinking is also said to be associative. All the dreams and delusion can be a part of withdrawal behavior where the individual tries to escape from their reality. Instead of facing the demands of their reality, they escape in fantasies which leave them non-directed and unconnected to what is around them.

Daydreaming is considered a very normal type of behavior, but when a person indulges in too many and becomes delusional, it is definitely a problem. Delusional behavior is an abnormality that strays from normal thought processes. Such delusions can make a person think they are in another role different from their reality. A man with financial issues can be deluded into thinking he is a millionaire. Someone who works a normal clerk job can think of himself as a great artist. These delusions can take any form and allow the person to escape from the reality of their situation. Sometimes these delusions can have such a grip on the mental state of the person that a perfectly healthy person thinks of himself as suffering from a chronic disease and experiences the symptoms in his mind.

Development of Thinking

A person's ability to learn things and to solve problems is dependent on their ability to think clearly. This will help them in adjusting to the demands of life and live successfully. The thought process of a person plays a definitive role in his development. If a person wants to be able to contribute something to society, his thinking has to be careful, distinct and constructive. Only then can he be capable of worthwhile contribution. People have to develop their thinking process by acquiring more knowledge and practicing a proper process of thinking. There are certain methods that help in this development process.

1. Sufficient knowledge and experience play a big role in systematic thinking. This is important to consider while raising children; they need to be provided with an adequate amount of these to help them. Children have to be trained so that they can be more perceptive and sensitive

to all thoughts and experiences. This will help to develop their process of critical thinking as well. Every individual has to be provided with sufficient opportunities to experience more. They need to practice self-study and participate in activities that are stimulating.

2. Motivation is important to mobilize thinking energy. Motivation generates genuine interest and attention in the thinking process. This helps in improving efficiency while thinking and increases adequacy as well. It is important to think in definite lines and aim for a definite purpose. Every problem we think about should be connected to immediate needs or motives.

3. There has to be enough freedom and flexibility for thinking. Unnecessary obstructions or restrictions will restrict the thought process. If what you already know does not help you to solve a problem, think of new ways. Narrowing your field of thought can be limiting for the development of your thinking.

4. Another method that is useful while facing hard problems is incubation. Sometimes it is hard to

find a solution no matter how much you think about it. At this time, you should set the problem aside and engage in some other activity. During this period of rest, your brain may actually end up giving you an answer to your question. This is how the incubation method works.

5. Each person also has to have proper ideas about concepts. Concepts encompass a lot of ideas, objects, or events. Concept formation has to begin in the early years. Language development is just as crucial. Thinking depends upon language and how the person is able to articulate their thoughts. Language can be in written or spoken form, but everyone has to have a good handle on it. All the words, symbols, signs, etc. used to act as tools during the thought process, if a person's language development is insufficient, they cannot move towards effective thinking. Development of concepts and language is required for an efficient thought process. Improper development of these can hamper the person's

progress and cause many issues that can affect their lives.

6. The reasoning process that a person adopts influences his thinking. Incorrect thoughts arise from illogical reasoning. Cultivating the habit of logical reasoning is important. Logic will help the person reason and think correctly.

Thinking tools

Thinking tools are some of the elements that are used in the thinking process:

1. Images of people, objects, situations, etc. can all be developed in mind. Mental images are manipulated by the way a person thinks. They symbolize real-life situations or things. Thinking allows you to manipulate these mental images.

2. Concepts are general ideas of all objects or events in a general class. A concept can be used to economize the effort of thinking about something. If you hear of a single word, you will think of what that thing really is but also

think about your experiences or how it is associated with you personally.

3. Symbols or signs are also tools used to represent objects, activities, etc. There are symbols all around us that we use to represent certain things generally. Such symbolic expressions then stimulate your thoughts and result in you deciding how to act accordingly.

4. One of the most effective tools for thinking is language. It is the most highly developed instrument that allows people to carry out their thought process. Any language that a person learns helps them to listen, speak or read in it. This stimulates their thinking and development through it. This is why reading or writing acts as stimulants of the thinking process.

5. Taking part in activities that require muscle movement can also be helpful. There is a positive relation between thinking and muscular activities. Greater muscle tension is related to the more intensive thought process, and it applies conversely as well.

6. The main function of the brain is to think. This is why the mind is said to be the core tool of the thought process. Any experiences that our sense organs go through cannot be stimulating or work for our thought process unless the brain cells receive the signals and interpret them. Every mental image can only be used after the brain processes it and only then can you reconstruct them. The functioning of your brain is responsible for most of your thought process, and it would not be possible without the brain.

Automatic Intrusive Thoughts

Thoughts come in and go out of our mind all the time. These thoughts might be utterly unrelated to what you are doing at the time or where you are. You could be thinking about what you ate for lunch during class. Such random thoughts can occur in any unrelated situations. These types of thoughts can be of two types. One is like the above that is harmless and has no negative impact on you. The second instance is when the thoughts are negative and might incite maladaptive behavior. Automatic and intrusive thoughts are those that seem to suddenly come into your mind from nowhere. These kinds of thoughts can cause a surge of many different emotions like fear or sadness in the person. It can cause you to worry about things that have not happened yet or might never even happen, but you will still keep thinking about it. It can also make you think of a situation that might occur in the future, but you feel extremely grief ridden in the present.

The point is, these thoughts are sudden and involuntary and can lead to undesirable behavior. Automatic intrusive thoughts are a part of how addicts might think. They might be clean for a while but the sudden thought that they can try one more time might come into their head. Giving in to these kinds of thoughts is the undesirable behavior that you need to avoid. For addicts, it can cause a relapse that can even be fatal. When these thoughts come into an addict's mind, they cannot seem to shake it off or think of something else.

There are many reasons for why these kinds of sudden thoughts pop into someone's mind. It can be due to any trigger that plays a part in their addiction or illness. For addicts, the trigger could be a situation that prompts them to escape from reality. It could also just be the sight of someone related to his or her life of drugs. Sometimes, these thoughts pop back in your head just because you are trying too hard to suppress or ignore them.

If the thought of someone close to you dying keeps popping in your head, it will make you very sad every time. Some people are extremely sensitive and cannot process these kinds of thoughts or push them away. They might start crying right then even though the other person is living a perfectly healthy life at the time. But the thought of the loss that might come later seems too unbearable and they keep worrying about it.

As you can see, these sudden intrusive thoughts can have a very negative impact on your life. It is essential to identify these thoughts and deal with them before you act on the maladaptive reaction it could lead you to. Negative feelings are also in the stream of normal emotion, but they have to be in such a limit that you can process them healthily. If there are too many negative feelings in a person's mind, it can lead to unwanted behavior that could harm them or even another person. Instead of ignoring or trying to suppress such negative thoughts, you have to learn to process and deal with them. In this way, they will pass and not be stuck in your head. For instance, if a particular thought causes you to worry, analyze it. Think about the facts that are related to it; has it happened yet? Is there any indication that it is about to happen soon?

When you understand that there is no real need to worry, you can get rid of the thought and pacify your mind. You also need to learn to accept some things. For instance, the loss of a loved one who is old or incurably ill is inevitable. Worrying and obsessing over it will not change the situation. Grief is a normal emotion but let it come when it happens. Don't try to fight the inevitable and don't let these kinds of thoughts control you. Think of positive things when you feel such unnecessary negative thoughts popping up in your head. If something bad happens in the morning, don't keep thinking that the whole day is going to be bad. Just let go of it and try to go through the rest of the day typically. Holding on to negativity is counterproductive to your mental health.

Although it is easy to say such things, we know that it is harder to put them in practice. Learning to manage these intrusive thoughts is a process that takes time, but it will benefit you in the long run. It is essential to make an effort and not let negative emotions control and overtake our minds. Sometimes these thoughts can be extremely out of control, and that is where therapists can help you out. They can study and diagnose your problem and help in healing your mind. Intrusive thoughts can be a symptom of extreme distress or anxiety and need to be given due attention.

The process of thinking, reasoning or problem-solving in each person is affected by various factors. It is influenced by your habit of perceiving certain situations. Every person's experiences and perceptions from the past set a path for their way of thinking. This is why we can sometimes make mistakes in our conclusions when our thoughts are biased due to any likes, dislikes, prejudices, etc. The set way of thinking influenced by the past can hinder correct and effective thinking and lead to ineffective behavior.

If your thinking is not based on the information, then it can be incorrect and even harmful. Biases or prejudices do not allow you to be logical in your reasoning process. You can easily draw wrong conclusions when your thinking is based on these factors. It makes you ignore facts that support the right solution and instead reach the wrong conclusion. There are many reasons that can lead to errors in thought. When we let ourselves get swayed by our emotions, it can affect our thinking. For instance, fear of failure can affect a person's performance in an exam. Incorrect thinking also results from the inability to look at a problem from different angles. A broad viewpoint is needed to take everything into account.

Superstitions and a set belief system also affect your way of thinking. If you depend on these and not accurate information, then it will inadvertently lead to the wrong results or conclusions. This will be inhibitory to your growth process and the development of your thinking process. Unscientific thinking can cause a conflict of interest with facts and the truth. Wishful thinking or delusions can result in errors of thought as well. These kinds of thoughts can be dangerous or even fatal.

The Voices in your Head

Every time you are about to do something, does it feel like a voice in your head stops you from doing it? Does it feel like there is a constant war going on between you and the voice in your head? Here we will talk about these and how you can stop yourself from becoming a victim to these.

Most people with mental issues suffer a lot due to negative thinking. Negative thoughts lie at the core of so many issues that can easily be dealt with otherwise. In reality, negative thinking is wired into your brain to let you decipher what is wrong and protect yourself; it is a survival tool. But when these negative thoughts get out of control, they can create a different reality and don't just help you differentiate situations. People who have anxiety or suffer from depression are a prime example of this.

Someone who is depressed always has a focus on what is wrong in their lives or their past. They feel ashamed or guilty for what they may have done. Anxiety causes some people to fear what hasn't even happened yet. Both of these are a negative type of focus of thoughts. Chronic negative thinking causes depression and can make you numb to everything and all emotions including love or fear. There are negative voices in your head, which hold you back and don't allow you to progress in life. It is important to fight those voices and manage them before they take control of your life.

One of the common voices in a depressed person's head tells them that they don't deserve to be loved. This voice can stem from different incidents like a breakup. It makes you think that the breakup happened because of you and you keep blaming yourself. This same voice will create a pattern of thought that makes you feel unloved and undeserving of love at all times. It will give you illogical reasoning and convince you in a way that your self-esteem takes a huge hit, and you believe this voice blindly. If you listen to this voice for too long, it will cause you stop taking care of yourself, and you won't let others do it either. This pattern can lead to substance abuse where the person seeks solace from their emotions. This type of thinking can often result in people staying stuck in bad relationships. Even when they get out of one bad one, they enter another and reason that they deserve it or convince themselves that they don't deserve something better. You need to fight back this belief by using positive affirmations and telling yourself that you deserve love just like every other person in the world. Before focusing on giving love to others, you have to push away that voice in your head and learn to love yourself and receive it as well. Take care of yourself in every way possible and show yourself some self-love.

Another negative voice that gets stuck in the head of many people is the voice of regret. They are stuck in their past and what they failed to achieve at some point. They keep holding on to the regret of things they did not do or did do. These thoughts keep coming into their mind, and it keeps them stuck in an unproductive cycle. If you keep listening to the voice of regret, then you give it power over you to stop you from doing better in your present. You have to accept regret as an emotion, and it has to pass. You cannot hold on to it and obsess over it forever. You might regret that one thing but holding on to regret will lead to many more regrets down the line. Instead, use reaffirmation to tell yourself that you need to trust the process, and something good will come out of it all. Instead of wallowing in regret, you can think about what it is you regret and maybe try to correct the situation now. Identify the goal you wanted to achieve and try to achieve it now if you regretted not doing it earlier. If you regret the way you behaved towards someone, apologize to them and make sure you don't do it again.

Don't keep regretting and punishing yourself. Transform the negative thoughts into a positive reality.

Another voice that gets stuck in your head may tell you that you are not ready for something that you really want or need to do. You need to realize that you or anyone else is never 100% ready for all the things that they go through in life. If it is something that you want to do, just go for it. Don't overthink or talk yourself out of it. That voice in your head has probably been telling you that you are not ready for a long time now, but you are. The results can be good or bad, but you will never know unless you try. Waiting for the right moment will just keep you stuck in a loop where you never get things done. Opportunities will not always come by. If you let them pass by you, at some point, you will see that you have lost all your chances. That little voice in your head will not help you, and it will turn into a voice of regret that will keep gnawing at you. Even if you don't feel you are half as ready as you should be, fight with the percentage that works in your favor. There will be many decisions in your life that you will have to make in the spur of the moment. You won't always get the chance to think them through or analyze them. You have to trust your gut and make some spur of the moment decisions and just pray things to work out. More often than not, you will see that they turn out okay. It might not be perfect but okay is also good. Getting out there will help in cultivating more experiences and build your character. Stopping yourself from doing things on the basis of fear and a negative voice in your head will get you nowhere. Use an affirmation thought telling yourself that you are ready and enough at every point in your life. You need to build your self-confidence in order to stand strong and face things head-on. You can always grow as a person, but you have what it takes to get there so don't doubt it. If you don't trust yourself, how can others have confidence in you either?

How changing your thought process can change your life

Changing your thoughts can accordingly help to change your life. It might sound far-fetched but trust us when we say it is true. Negative thoughts will result in negative energy in your life. It will cause you to stay stuck in a rut where you can't get things done and are not happy. Negative thoughts will hinder your growth as a person and cause problems like anxiety, depression, etc. Positive thoughts have the opposite effect and are obviously a power tool. However, you will be surprised with how most people allow negative thoughts to control them instead of positive thoughts that will benefit them.

You can take advantage of the fact that thoughts can change your life for the better. Your thought process plays a crucial role in who you are, what you do, what happens around you, etc. You can improve it for the better to see positive changes in your life. Constantly thinking about problems will stop you from making use of all the opportunities that come your way and can actually help you solve your problems. Focusing on problems makes you think you are doomed for failure and you might not even try hard enough to deal with them. You will tend to avoid action or introspection of these situations. The negative thoughts will thus be mirrored in your actual life.

If you learn to control these negative thoughts, you can take a step in the right direction. You can start focusing on success and what you need to do to achieve it. Think about what you want from your life and focus on that. Don't think about what has gone wrong and how things never seem to work out for you. These kinds of thoughts will work as a negative reaffirmation and just make things worse. Positive affirmations will help things work out in a positive way.

Creating a mental image of what you want and who you want to be can be a useful tool. This allows you to envision the possibilities of what you can achieve and gives you a goal to work towards. Having no aim can make you wander aimlessly and allows your mind to tend towards negative, useless thoughts freely. Thinking about failures and hardships all the time just closes doors of opportunity for you. Instead, think of success and happiness, and you will be motivated to achieve them. Open yourself to more possibilities and take advantage of all the chances you get to change your life for the better. If you have financial issues and keep focusing on how difficult your life is, you are just wasting time and energy that you can use to earn real money. You are just wasting time by thinking of how hard your life is and keep reaffirming that you will stay in that same situation. Instead, if you clear your mind of these thoughts, you can focus on changing your situation. A successful person will be using their time and energy to set goals and get past any obstacles in their way. They don't sit and lament about all the hardships they might have to face on the way. They focus and believe that they will fulfill their ambitions.

Thoughts and perseverance can help anyone achieve what they want. You should try reading more about the law of attraction to understand that what you are is what you will attract. If you are a negative person, you will only attract negative outcomes in your life. If you are a good and positive person, you will automatically attract goodness in your life. Learn more about how you can use creative visualization to envision and achieve goals. Perseverance is the key to achieving anything. The process of changing your thoughts will not be an easy one either, but you need to decide on what you want and work towards it. If you expect quick results, you will usually just give up even before you get a chance to really begin. There are no shortcuts to great things, but the effort will get you there. If you really want changes in your life you have to invest the time and effort into it. Just reading all this alone will not be enough; you have to use the right techniques to change your mindset and also take the right actions. This way you will work towards improving yourself and your life for the better. Complaining and thinking negative thoughts will keep you in the same situations for a long time and prevent you from making any progress in your life.

If you want to change your life, you have to change your thoughts. Changing how you think will help to change how you feel and how you react to situations. It will have an impact on the actions you take. This inner change of positive thinking will result in positive changes in your external life as well.

Chapter 2

WHAT IS COGNITIVE BEHAVIORAL THERAPY?

In this chapter, we will explain what Cognitive behavioral therapy is and why people use it, and how they benefit from it. Cognitive behavioral therapy or CBT is a treatment pattern that aims to cure the effects of depression or any mental illness and also find a permanent solution by studying behavior or thinking patterns.

The main idea behind this therapy is that nearly all our actions have some thought process underlying them. Originally, CBT was designed to treat depression specifically, but over the years, it has been used expansively to treat many different kinds of mental health issues. The therapy is a type of psychosocial intervention that focuses on changing any negative behavior, thoughts or beliefs, improve emotional processing, and developing coping strategies.

The basic principles of behavioral as well as cognitive psychology are used in cognitive behavioral therapy. CBT focuses on problems and is oriented towards actions. It falls in the second wave of therapy and is different from the older approaches towards psychotherapy. Earlier, therapists used to study a person's behavior and look for the unconscious meaning behind them to diagnose the problem. CBT therapists are more focused on treating specific problems related to the mental disorder that a patient has been diagnosed with. They try to help the patient reach some goals using effective strategies that will help them and decrease their symptoms.

According to CBT, psychological disorders are related to thought distortions and maladaptive behavior. Teaching the patient coping mechanisms and other skills can reduce the symptoms and effects of the diagnosed diseases. One area of CBT was focused on changing maladaptive thinking to change the related behavior or effect on the patient. The other area that is more focused on these days emphasizes changing the patient's relationship with maladaptive thinking. CBT is not focused on diagnosing the patient and his disease but on finding as much of a solution as possible to benefit the patient.

Many studies have found that even without psychoactive medications, CBT is quite effective in treating milder forms of addictions, personality disorders, stress, depression, and anxiety. Therefore, doctors recommend a combination of medication with CBT to deal with more severe forms of these mental issues. Conditions like bipolar disorder, obsessive-compulsive disorder, major depression, etc. are treated using a combination of psychoactive medicines and CBT. Even children or adults with behavioral problems like aggression are recommended CBT to improve their behavior. Interpersonal psychotherapy and cognitive behavioral therapy are the only two psychosocial therapies that are compulsory for all psychiatry residents to train in.

Cognitive behavioral therapy involves cognitive therapy and behavior therapy. Let's try to understand these two types of individually.

Cognitive therapy

Aaron T. Beck was an American psychiatrist who first developed cognitive therapy. According to him a person's thoughts, feelings, and behavior are somehow interconnected to each other. Studying each of these aspects individually would not be an effective method of understanding a person's mental state accurately. Beck suggested the combined study of all three aspects to understand and diagnose a patient's condition. The appropriate treatment can be suggested only once this is done.

Behavior therapy

A person's state of mind is understood by studying their behavioral patterns. Using this information, the appropriate treatment is suggested. The purpose of behavior therapy is to treat a person by studying how they behave in different situations and respond to different stimuli. Sometimes their thoughts and feelings are also given attention to in this therapy, but the main focus is on actual behavior. The therapist subjects the person to all the situations that the patient would normally go through every day and studies their responses. They use this to try and understand what the cause of the problem is and try to solve it or find a way to deal with it for the patient.

Blending cognitive and behavior therapy is one of the best ways to treat patients using cognitive behavioral therapy. Using two different medical therapies properly together is much more beneficial for the patient. CBT emphasizes that logic or reason cannot be used to treat every disorder that affects the human mind. Sometimes you have to consider factors that defy logic as well. Medication can only go till a certain level. CBT and other therapies help in going the extra mile for proper treatment.

How to go about getting CBT?

When a person chooses to undergo CBT, a therapist will be assigned to that individual. A relationship needs to be established between these two people so that the patient can trust and allow the therapist to treat him appropriately. The therapist has to come in close contact with the person to understand his thoughts and behavior. They have to watch the person in their usual environment to study them properly. Regular sessions are conducted to allow the person to share their emotions and experiences with the therapist. You can go at your own pace as you choose to slowly open up to the therapist.

The therapy is taken step by step and allows the therapist to understand your mental state. CBT is a more direct approach than many other therapies and thus has better results. It focuses on the individual, and the treatment is more tailored according to their needs. The practical aspect of this therapy makes it much more effective than most methods used for mental health treatment.

There are six phases in mainstream CBT, and they are as follows:

- ❖ The first phase is the psychological assessment.
- ❖ The second phase is the reconceptualization.
- ❖ The third phase is skill acquisition.
- ❖ The fourth phase is the consolidation of skills and application training.
- ❖ The fifth phase involves generalization and maintenance.
- ❖ The final phase is the follow up on post-treatment assessment.

Kanfer and Saslow created these steps in a system for CBT. After the treatment is complete, the psychologist must assess if it worked for the patient or not. The decrease in the negatively-inclined behavior means that it was successful, but if it remains the same or their condition is aggravated, then the treatment failed.

CBT can be done in a group as well as individual settings. The term itself can refer to different types of interventions like goal setting, self-instruction, biofeedback, etc. Most of the techniques are adapted in a way that they can be applied for self-help. Some therapists may be more cognitively oriented while others will focus on behavioral therapy, but the entire process will include both.

History of CBT

Cognitive behavioral therapy has aspects that originated in different ancient philosophical traditions. Stoicism, in particular, is one from which CBT borrows its principles. Stoicism emphasized that any false beliefs that caused destructive emotions could be discarded by applying logic. This is the same as identifying cognitive distortions and treating them. Aaron T. Beck also referred to the origin of these thoughts in Stoic philosophy. Albert Ellis, John Stuart Mill, and Beck were some of the original endorsers of CBT for treatment of mental issues. Alfred Adler was one of the earliest therapists to talk of cognition in the field of psychotherapy. Albert Ellis was influenced by Adler's work and developed the REBT or rational emotive behavior therapy which is the earliest psychotherapy based on cognition. During this time, Aaron T. Beck started noticing that Freud's theory was not always applicable, and emotional distress could be the result of certain types of thoughts. He developed cognitive therapy from this and referred to such thoughts as automatic thoughts.

John B. Watson and Rayner conducted studies on conditioning around 1920, which were groundbreaking for behaviorism. Cognitive therapy developed around 1960, and behavior therapy can be traced to the early 1900s. Mary Cover Jones used behavioral therapy to study children in 1924. Joseph Wolfe further developed behavioral therapy in the 1950s using all these previously conducted studies. There were many more over the years who studied conditioning and behavior therapy, like Arnold Lazarus, Glenn Wilson, and Ivan Pavlov.

The theory put forward by John B. Watson, Clark L. Hull, and Ivan Pavlov inspired more study on the subject, and many researchers started using it in the United States, South Africa as well as the United Kingdom. Joseph Wolfe of Britain used behavioral research to treat neurotic disorders. His work was the early foundation of the fear reduction techniques that are used in the modern day.

Hans Eysenck promoted behavior therapy as an effective treatment, and at the same time, B.F. Skinner was working on operant conditioning. Later, Julian Rotter and Albert Bandura contributed with their work on social learning theory, and they demonstrated how cognition affects learning as well and behavior modification. The first wave of CBT was the emphasis on behavioral factors. The second wave was started by the REMT and cognitive therapy developed by Ellis and Beck.

The third wave of CBT developed from blending theory and technical applications of behavior therapy and cognitive therapy. Dialectical behavior therapy, acceptance, and commitment therapy are the most important therapies from the third wave of CBT.

Types of CBT

Let's take a look at the different types of cognitive behavioral therapy.

Brief cognitive behavioral therapy or BCBT

This is a form of CBT that was developed to deal with therapy that had time constraints. Usually, when BCBT is used for treatment, it takes around a total of 12 hours divided into a few sessions. David M. Rudd developed and implemented this technique to treat suicidal tendency in soldiers who were deployed overseas.

The first part of it is an orientation that involves a commitment to treatment, crisis response, safety planning, survival kits, reasons for the living card, a model of suicidal tendencies, treatment journal, means restriction, and lessons learned. The skill focus is on skill development worksheets, coping cards, demonstration, practice and, skill refinement. The third part is relapse prevention, which involves skill generalization and skill refinement.

Cognitive-emotional behavioral therapy or CEBT

CEBT was initially developed to treat those with eating disorders, but now it is used to treat many other problems like depression, PTSD, or even anger problems. CEBT uses dialectical behavioral therapy and cognitive behavioral therapy to help in understanding emotions and increase tolerance. This helps in the therapy and is often referred to as a pre-treatment for long-term therapy.

Structure cognitive behavioral training or SCBT

SCBT was developed with philosophies drawn from Cognitive behavior. It emphasizes that beliefs, emotions, and thoughts all are related to behavior. It also used Ellis's rational emotive behavior therapy and others to build on CBT. The only ways it is different from core CBT is that it has a much-regimented format, and it is a predetermined finite process. SCBT only becomes personalized from the input of the patient. This therapy was designed for getting specific results in limited time and has been used to treat addictive behavior related to substance abuse. Criminal psychology uses SCBT for recidivism reduction.

Moral reconation therapy

This therapy was developed to help treat antisocial personality disorder in felons. This helps in reducing the risk of them repeating their offenses in the future. Instead of one-on-one sessions, this therapy is conducted in groups. This is because it might otherwise reinforce narcissism in some felons. The group meetings are usually held once a week for about six months.

Stress inoculation training

This therapy is used to focus on stressors that affect patients. It uses cognitive and behavioral therapy with humanistic training for a blend that will benefit the patient. This therapy helps in coping with stress or anxiety issues and is a three-phase program. This therapy helps the individual to use their skills to adapt to the stressors.

The first phase of this therapy includes reading materials, psychological testing, and self-monitoring. This part of the process helps the therapist to create a program specifically for the individual. The second phase focuses on skills acquisition and continued conceptualization. Skills are taught to help the individual in dealing with the stressors that affect them and then these are practiced. It involves problem solving, communication, self-regulation, etc. The third phase involves a follow-through of the skills that were acquired in training. The individual gets the chance to use their skills on different stressors through role-play, imagery, etc. By the end of the training, the person will know how to break down their stressors and deal with them in the short term or long-term basis using their skills.

Mindfulness-based cognitive behavioral therapy

This therapy focuses on addressing subconscious tendencies and increasing awareness through a reflective approach. Three phases are used to achieve any goals that the individual sets.

Unified protocol

It is a form of the CBT that was developed at Boston University and is used to treat many depression and anxiety issues in patients, the unified protocol for trans-diagnostic treatment of emotional disorders gives the rationale that common underlying causes lead to most anxiety or depression disorders, and so they can be treated together. It involves psycho-education, cognitive reappraisal, emotion regulation, and changing behavior.

Pros and Cons of CBT

Just like everything else, CBT therapy has its pros and cons. The therapy can be found to be effective for many people but isn't necessarily suitable for all. Let's take a look at the disadvantages and advantages of cognitive behavioral therapy.

Pros:

- There are some mental illnesses where medication alone is not sufficient for treatment. CBT has been found to be helpful here, and along with medication, it helps in better treatment for the patient.
- If you compare CBT to other talking therapies, it is completed in a much shorter period of time which is an advantage.
- CBT is a very structured type of therapy, and this means that it can be provided through different means like books, apps, and one on one sessions or group therapy.
- It teaches strategies that are practical and can be used in everyday life even after the therapy is completed.

Cons:

- The therapy will not work unless the patient cooperates with the therapist. The therapist can only advise and help to a limit, after that your effort is necessary.

❖ It can take a lot of your time to attend the therapy sessions and also carry out the exercises in between sessions recommended by the therapist.
❖ The therapy may not be suitable for those who have special needs and learning difficulties.
❖ It might make you uncomfortable since you have to confront anxieties and emotions that make you uncomfortable.
❖ It focuses singularly on the person's capability to change their thoughts and behavior. It does not factor-in or work on external factors like other people who affect a person's mental health.
❖ It can also be a problem when CBT does not address issues of the past that deserve attention. This is because the therapy is too focused on the present.

Differences between CBT and other psychotherapies:

There are a few noticeable differences between this therapy and other psychotherapies that are practiced while treating mental health issues:

- ❖ CBT is pragmatic and identifies specific problems and allows the patient to solve them on their own.
- ❖ CBT is much more structured than other psychotherapies, which allow the patient to freely discuss their life and thoughts. CBT is focused on specific problems and goals.
- ❖ Other therapies often involve discussion and analysis of past experiences to help the patient. CBT disregards the past and focuses only on current problems faced by the patient.
- ❖ Other therapists might tell you what to do, and you would have to follow their instructions blindly. CBT is more of teamwork between the patient and the therapist, so they need to work together to find the solutions.

Chapter 3

COGNITIVE DISTORTION AWARENESS

In this chapter, we will learn about cognitive disorders, their symptoms, the effects of these disorders, and the most common cognitive distortion.

What are cognitive disorders?

Disorders that affect a person's cognitive abilities such as learning or memory are called cognitive disorders. These disorders can affect the cognitive function of the person in a way that it impairs their ability to stay in a normal environment. Cognitive disorders usually begin slowly and are not that noticeable, but over time they can seriously affect the quality of life of the individual.

Understanding and identifying a cognitive disorder will help in reducing the symptoms and treating the condition. Dementia, amnesia, motor skill disorders, and developmental disorders are some of the common cognitive disorders seen in people. One of the more prominently affecting cognitive disorders is Alzheimer's disease that affects millions of people around the world.

A variety of factors can cause cognitive disorders in people. Some people acquire these through genetics while others may be affected due to hormonal imbalances while they were in the womb. Environmental factors also play a role in the development of cognitive disorders. This can be due to improper nutrition while the child is in the womb as well. Substance abuse is another cause along with physical injuries that can cause a cognitive disorder to develop. Cognitive dysfunction may result from damage to certain areas of the brain that are responsible for cognitive functions. This can be due to physical trauma or the effect of drugs and alcohol on the brain.

Symptoms of cognitive disorders

The signs of a cognitive disorder may vary according to the condition, but a few common symptoms are observed in most cases. Some of these include confusion, impaired judgment, and confusion about identity, motor coordination issues, or even loss of memory. The symptoms of a cognitive disorder can be subtle initially, but the severity increases over time with the progression of the disease. One of the prime examples of this is Alzheimer's disease where the patient starts becoming forgetful about small things during early onset.

As the disease progresses over time, the person's memory can become severely impaired. Initially, they forget a few names or what they did the previous day. Later, they fail to recognize their loved ones and lose track of time as well. They might have some moments of clarity where everything seems normal again, but these pass and a confused state persists. It is important to pay attention to the early symptoms to help the patient as much as possible in fighting such diseases.

Physical symptoms include lack of motor coordination and unusual mannerisms. The person will tend to look confused or dazed most of the time. You might notice abnormal posture or problems in the balance as well.

Other than the symptoms stated above, an emotional imbalance is also observed in cognitive disorders. People who suffer from these conditions are prone to getting frustrated and emotional outbursts. This kind of emotional imbalance can be hard for the people around them to deal with. While some people have aggravated emotions, others might become numb and act emotionless. The reactions can differ in people.

Effects of cognitive disorders

Cognitive dysfunctions can cause short-term as well as long-term effects. Short-term effects like memory loss or a confused state are common. Long-term effects include forgetfulness, emotional instability, loss of memory, lack of control, etc. All of these affect the way of life of a person suffering from cognitive disorders.

Treatment

Various options for treatment of cognitive issues are available. Most cognitive disorders cannot be treated permanently, but the quality of life can be improved using drugs and treatments. Many drugs or supplements have been generated to help patients deal with cognitive dysfunctions like memory loss. Associated issues like depression or anxiety can also be treated using antidepressants and other drugs. Antidepressants are one of the most commonly used drugs for people with cognitive disorders.

Drugs are also used to help retain memory as much as possible for the person. A medical assessment helps the doctor to prescribe the appropriate drugs for any patient. However, such medications also come with some side effects that need to be kept in mind. Side effects include drowsiness and insomnia. The doctor will usually keep a close eye to check the effects of a particular medication on an individual and determine if it is helping them.

Suffering from cognitive dysfunctions can be extremely hard for a person. It makes them frustrated and irritable when they realize how the disease is affecting their lives. It has a negative effect on their mental stability, and this can lead to maladaptive behavior. Some people may look for control over their situation through means like drugs or alcohol abuse. Because of the lack of control that comes with these conditions, patients look for a way to assert control-using drugs like stimulants that improve mental functioning.

Self-prescription of these doses is a common abuse. There are also cases of an overdose on such medications. Some patients increase the dosage by themselves if they feel like the prescribed dosage is not helping them. This can be quite dangerous and even fatal. Having too many of these drugs over time, the person can become dependent on these medications and even suffer from withdrawal symptoms when they try to get off them. Medical supervision is required to help patients recover from such symptoms.

Cognitive disorders are quite often linked with addictions in patients. Due to this, many types of research even say that addiction is a type of cognitive dysfunction. Substance abuse itself can be the cause of some types of cognitive impairments. ADHD is very commonly prevalent amongst alcoholics, and they are more prone to it.

Common cognitive distortions

Cognitive distortions are ways in which your mind may convince you of things that are not true. Inaccurate thoughts linked to negative thinking arise in your mind, and you feel like they are accurate and make sense. However, these are irrational thoughts that only make you feel bad about yourself. Such cognitive distortions play a major role in your behavior. It is important to identify these cognitive distortions to refute the negative thinking and replace it with more balanced thoughts.

Some of the more common cognitive distortions are as follows:

1. Mental filtering is one of the cognitive distortions that make a person focus on negative details and magnify them. Instead of focusing on reality, it allows the person to only see the negative aspect of everything and block out the positive
2. Another distortion is polarized thinking which makes the person feel like things either have to

be perfect or totally wrong. This does not allow them to be satisfied with any gray area and accept that some things may go wrong. Thinking in black and white can make situations seem extreme.

3. Another problem is generalizing based on a single fact or an incident. The person may feel defeated with everything even if they fail at one single instance. For instance, a student failing one test will conclude that his whole semester will be bad and that he should just quit.

4. Jumping to conclusions can be another distorted behavior. The person might think that another person is holding a grudge against them or hates them just because of a single unpleasant encounter. They might also conclude what their future will hold based on a single instance.

5. Some people tend to believe that something really bad will happen and it is inevitable. They will always assume the worst in a situation and believe that it will turn out badly.

6. Another distortive behavior is when the person takes everything personally. They always think that what another person does or says is somehow connected to them or directed towards them. They think of themselves as the center of everything and everyone's life around them.
7. Another distortion is where they feel like no one is fair to them. They often feel resentful and angry whenever things don't go their way.
8. Blaming others for what happens in your life or for your feelings is another type of distortive behavior. The situation could also be reversed, and instead, they blame everything on themselves. There is no rationale for the reasoning behind all the blaming, but it is always focused in one direction in an unhealthy way.
9. Emotional reasoning is another tendency that can be problematic. The person believes that everything that they feel is valid and true. Emotions can be very strong and take over

rational thinking. Emotional reasoning can be an unhealthy way of reflecting on situations.

10. Another distortive tendency is to expect changes in others according to what you think they need to change. This is commonly seen in relationships where one partner expects the other to change because they believe it is for their better and only then will they be perfect.

11. Labeling is another unhealthy habit that can be quite a hindrance. The person will generalize and label another person based on a single negative quality. It can also be applied to themselves where they generalize themselves as a failure if they fail at one single thing. This kind of labeling can be very judgmental and offensive.

12. Some people also have the problem of thinking that they are always right and feel the need to prove that the other person is wrong. They do not consider that they can be wrong sometimes and go to huge lengths to emphasize that they are right. They usually disregard the truth or

others' feelings and only righteously look at themselves.

Cognitive behavioral therapy alone with medications can help in the treatment of these distortive symptoms. It helps the patient identify their negative behavior and teaches them to improve their perspective. CBT also helps them in practicing more positive thoughts and improving their distortive symptoms.

Depression is linked to any cognitive symptoms like these. It makes the depressed person think negatively and associate every situation with a negative outcome. It is vital to teach these individuals to think more positively. They are first taught to monitor all negative thoughts using tools like a journal. Then they are taught to challenge and rationalize these thoughts to replace them with better thoughts. There are many steps involved, but ultimately treatment and medication can help improve distortive conditions to a noticeable extent.

Chapter 4

COGNITIVE RESTRUCTURING

Cognitive distortions are usually just like any bad habit, and they can be changed for the better with time and practice. An important part of CBT is cognitive restructuring. It is a process that teaches the individual to identify and refute all maladaptive thoughts. Strategies like thought recording, guided imagery, and Socratic questioning are used in cognitive restructuring. Some other commonly used methods include reattribution cognitive rehearsal and listing rational alternatives. The goal of cognitive restructuring is to help the individual change stressful thought patterns to a less stress-inducing way of thinking.

The cognitive restructuring was initially developed as a part of CBT and REBT. This technique has helped many people learn to cope better with stressful situations and thoughts. It is a little difficult to implement it by yourself, but with assistance from a therapist, the technique can be quite useful.

There are four steps involved in cognitive restructuring:

1. The first step is to identify any automatic intrusive thoughts that cause the person to think negatively.
2. The second step is to identify the cognitive distortions associated with these negative thoughts identified in step one.
3. The third step is to rationally dispute all such negative automatic thoughts.
4. The fourth step is to develop rational rebuttals of such thoughts.

Take some time and start noticing whenever you have any cognitive distortion. Take notice of any time where you find yourself thinking negatively and jumping to negative conclusions. Then ask yourself how you can change your view about that situation. Think of the positive outcomes possible instead of any negative outcome that you predicted. Think of what the most realistic outcome could be.

Use a journal to mark down every time you over-think a situation and write if those thoughts helped in solving any problem. Do these for a few days and at the end, check how many times the over-thinking helped you in any way. You should also start marking down your daily routine and rate your productivity level every day. Compare your productivity level every few weeks.

When you have a negative thought, evaluate it. Write down any evidence that supports the negative thought and write down what proves that you are wrong. Keep trying this to rationalize what thoughts are valid and true.

Mindfulness meditation also helps in focusing your attention to the present. Every time you think of something negative, try and bring your attention back to something like your breathing. You also need to reduce self-criticism and be more compassionate towards yourself. If you do something wrong or silly, talk kindly to yourself and acknowledge your wrongdoing as part of human experience. This will also help you to think more kindly about others over time.

Cognitive restricting will help you to learn how you can stop listening to your automatic thoughts and test them for accuracy. It involves evaluation of the thoughts that come into your mind and learning how to change them for the better. Asking yourself some questions will help you in the process. Think about any evidence that supports your thoughts and what doesn't. Question yourself to find out if you are underestimating yourself and your coping abilities. Think of the worst possible scenarios and compare them to your current situation.

After the process of cognitive restructuring, think of your original thoughts again and rephrase them to be more accurate and not distorted. With some practice and patience, you will be able to change all your stress-inducing thoughts and feel better.

Chapter 5

DEPRESSION & ANXIETY

Depression

Do you often feel "down" or experience "the blues"? Most people talk about it casually and don't give much thought to this kind of feeling. You might think it is entirely normal and it is but to a limit. Your entire life will at some point or the other, cause you to encounter situations where you feel sad or rejected. Unrealistic expectations from the people around you will create a sense of disappointment and rejection that can sometimes be overwhelming. It is normal to feel sad about certain things for a while, but if you feel low most of the time, then you might be suffering from depression.

Depression makes you feel sad, lose interest in things, and feel low persistently as you go about your daily life. These are all feelings that everyone experiences, but if they persist for too long, it can affect your mental and physical health. Studies conducted have shown that nearly 8 percent of the population suffers from depression and this includes all people over 12. The scale somehow seems to be increasing over the years, but not enough attention is paid to mental health even now.

The World Health Organization stated that depression is the most common disease that ails people worldwide and at least 300 million people are affected by it all over the world. You might feel like you are alone or even be ashamed to admit this illness, but you have no cause to. It is actually more common than you realize and can be treated.

Depression is more common among women than it is among men. It makes you lose interest in things that you previously enjoyed, and you feel unable to find joy in anything at all. Depression is different from grieving like during the death of a loved one. Differentiating depression from mood fluctuations is crucial. A temporary response to a situation that makes you sad is not the same as being depressed. However, depression can result from the bereavement for a loved one. It is not easy to understand the real causes of depression, and there is no single reason. It involves genetic, environmental, biological, and psychological factors.

Depression is diagnosed by consulting a doctor or specialist. Seeking the help of a health professional for mental illness is just as important as it is for physical illness. Don't assume that you can work everything out on your own. You must reach out for help. A professional will evaluate your condition, find the cause, and recommend the best treatment for your benefit. The assessment can also include a physical medical check-up to rule out all possible causes that can be linked to your physical health as well. Doctors also use questionnaires to assess how severe the depression is and to learn more about the patient. One of the most commonly used tools for rating depression is the Hamilton scale.

Symptoms of depression

- ❖ Lack or reduction of interest in activities you previously loved.

- ❖ Slow movement and speech.
- ❖ Feeling low all the time.
- ❖ Abnormal sleeping patterns like insomnia or hypersomnia.
- ❖ Lack of energy or fatigue.
- ❖ Feeling guilty or worthless all the time.
- ❖ Lack of concentration.
- ❖ Inability to think clearly.
- ❖ Thoughts of suicide or death.
- ❖ Lack of appetite and weight loss.
- ❖ Lack of sexual desire.

Types of depression

Depression is quite difficult to endure, and it is a risk factor for several chronic conditions like heart diseases and dementia. Certain depressive symptoms can occur due to various reasons. If you or anyone you know is experiencing any mood swings or any cognitive changes for more than a couple of weeks, then it's a good idea to consult your medical practitioner about it. There are four common types of depression, and they are major depression, bipolar disorder, seasonal affective disorder, and persistent disorder.

Major depression is a classic type of depression. In this state, the mood of the person going through it will be quite dark and all-consuming. The individual might also lose interest in all activities including the ones that they used to enjoy. They may experience insomnia, difficulty in sleeping, weight loss, loss of appetite, and a general feeling of worthlessness. Thoughts of death, as well as suicide, are commonly reported. Psychotherapy and medication are the usual modes of treatment.

Dysthymia is now known as persistent depressive disorder. It refers to the sort of depression that's characterized by spells of low mood. It can last for as long as two years before it transforms into a major depression. People who are diagnosed with this form of depression are capable of going through their daily lives but tend to feel quite low and joyless most of the time. The other symptoms include loss of appetite, sleep changes, consistently low levels of energy and low self-esteem.

Bipolar disorder was originally known as manic-depressive disorder and those who suffer from this condition experience bouts of depression. Their mood oscillates between periods of happiness or exceptionally high energy and periods of absolute depression. The common symptoms that characterize this form of depression are quite the opposite those of general depression. The symptoms of bipolar disorder include grand ideas, unrealistic high self-esteem, reduction in the need for sleep, ability to process things at a great speed, indulging in activities to attain extreme pleasure and even overspending. Terrible bouts of depression follow spells of extreme happiness. A person having bipolar disorder can experience the highest of highs and the lowest of lows. Medication is the most effective way to treat this disorder.

The seasonal affective disorder usually occurs when the days tend to grow shorter like in autumn and winter. This change in mood seems to be the result of the alterations in the daily rhythms of the body, the sensitivity to light, or even the way in which serotonin and melatonin function in the body.

Causes of depression

No definitive cause can be explained as the reason for depression. It develops as a result of a combination of factors like genetics, environment, biological factors, and social factors. However, some people are more at risk due to specific reasons than others, such as:

- Issues with friends or family like divorce.
- Medical concerns like a chronic illness or stress.
- Death of a loved one.
- Personality traits like low self-esteem or lack of self-confidence. Less ability to successfully cope with situations.
- Experiencing a traumatic childhood or incident.
- Substance abuse like drug addiction, alcoholism, etc.
- Having relatives with depression.
- Prescription drug abuse.

- ❖ Chronic pain syndrome.
- ❖ Head injury in the past.

All of the above increase the risk of an individual to suffer from depression and should be kept in mind.

Treatments for depression

Three components are involved in treating depression. The first is getting support from family and everyone around you. Let your family know what you are suffering from and help them understand it. They will help and support you through the process. Also, seek the support of professionals for your treatment. The second phase involves undergoing psychotherapy using therapies like cognitive behavioral therapy. This will help to understand and alleviate the symptoms of depression. The third component involves antidepressant medicines to treat your condition.

Psychotherapy is used as the first option when the case is not too severe. Therapies like CT or interpersonal psychotherapy depression can be quite beneficial and effective for the patient. These are the two most commonly used treatments for treating depression. CBT can be used in one on one sessions or in a group depending on the individual and therapist.

Antidepressants are used when the depression is much more severe. At that point, psychotherapy alone is not enough. Drugs are not recommended for treating children with depression and are prescribed with caution. There are different classes of antidepressants that act on different neurotransmitters. It is important to use drugs only according to a doctor's prescription, or you can make your condition even worse. Continue the drugs even after you see improvement in your condition if your doctor recommends it. This is to prevent any chances of a relapse. The treatment of depression is a long process that you need to stay patient about. Always consult a doctor when you start or stop antidepressants.

Amongst other treatments, patients are advised to partake in some regular exercise to increase the endorphin levels in the body. This will stimulate the nor-epinephrine, which is a neurotransmitter that affects mood.

Brain stimulation therapies like electroconvulsive therapy are also used to treat depression.

Anxiety

Do you experience intense feelings of fear and worry? Even in everyday situations where you don't need to feel such persistent worry, you start breathing heavily and your heart rate increases. These are all signs of anxiety. In some stressful situations, anxiety can be a very normal reaction. Certain situations make most people uncomfortable when they are not used to them. However, if it becomes an all-consuming feeling in your daily life, there is reason to worry. Anxiety disorder can be a tough condition to live with. It overwhelms your mind and body and leaves you feeling tired. Thankfully, it can be treated just like depression. CBT is a useful type of psychotherapy to treat anxiety as well.

Some people suffer from extreme social anxiety, which usually makes them feel awkward and uncomfortable when there are a lot of people around them. They channel negative thoughts, causing them to feel like they are weird and inadequate. To push away these feelings, such people often resort to drinking or drugs. This maladaptive coping will only cause more problems and can prove to be fatal. CBT can help such anxiety disorders by teaching the person to refute such negative thoughts and develop more positive thinking. Healthy coping mechanisms are taught to reduce stress and help them feel calm in such anxiety-inducing situations. CBT has helped many people defeat anxiety disorders and lead a more normal life.

Causes of anxiety:

- ❖ Panic disorders lead to anxiety, heart palpitations and dizziness.
- ❖ Phobias.
- ❖ Stress factors like relationships, work, finances, etc.

- ❖ Anxiety also stems from having to deal with a medical illness that is chronic and takes a toll on ordinary life.
- ❖ Generalized anxiety disorder.
- ❖ Side effects of certain medications also cause anxiety.

Some skills from CBT used to combat anxiety are as follows:

- ❖ The person is taught to have more tolerance for uncertainty. Some people who are unable to deal with the uncertainty of a situation get anxious over it. Learning to accept and be more tolerant can be very beneficial.
- ❖ They are also taught to notice when they keep thinking the same worrisome thoughts again and again, but it does not help them. Overthinking will reduce the ability to deal with a situation.
- ❖ They are also taught to recognize thought distortions like the prediction of adverse outcomes. The person has to identify such thoughts and rationalize them out. This way it

can help them change the thoughts more positively.

❖ Anxiety can also be dealt with using mindfulness techniques. It helps to cope with the situation instead of avoiding it and also control over-thinking negative thoughts.

CBT works similarly for both anxiety and depression and helps the individual to lead a happier life.

Chapter 6

JOURNALING

Do you remember writing a diary as a kid or even when you are in high school? You probably gave the diary a name and treated it as your confidant. You could share whatever you did the whole day and your feelings about things without worrying about any judgment. You just had to write it all down and feel better. Most people grow out of this habit as they get older and become embarrassed to even put words to such thoughts in their head. There is a fear of someone else coming across such thoughts in your diary. This habit can be beneficial and should be continued. In psychology, it is called journaling.

Therapists recommend journaling to patients as a part of their therapy. You can write down your thoughts and feelings every day, and this will help you understand them better. Keeping a journal can also be very beneficial in the treatment of issues like depression, stress or anxiety. The process helps you see things more clearly and regain control of your emotions. It is always better to find an outlet for negative emotions rather than suppressing and keeping them in. A journal is one tool you can use for this purpose.

Effective journaling is a tool that can help an individual to set goals, meet them and improve the general quality of life. It can be different for different people, but the outcome is usually positive for everyone. There are many different reasons that make journaling effective. Writing can help you to clear your head, connect your thoughts and feelings and analyze them. It also helps you to deal with negative thoughts and turn them into positive ones.

You might be doubtful about how journaling benefits mental health but trust us when we say it does. Many therapists have used this as a tool, and a lot of research also supports this. This simple practice of writing down your feelings and thoughts helps in striving towards a healthy mindset. Journaling has helped people boost their mood, improve memory, feel better, reduce depression symptoms, and reduce automatic thoughts.

People with PTSD post-traumatic stress disorder have found journaling to be a very useful practice. The writing helps them to confront emotions that they might otherwise suppress. It helps them to process any difficult events they went through. As they write, they create a sort of narrative of events that helps to put things in perspective for them. The patient has to confront the events and emotions related to their trauma and thus deal with it. Suppressing and ignoring the situation is detrimental to health.

You do not need to suffer from PTSD to benefit from journaling. In general, it helps people to improve mental wellbeing. You become more aware of what you do and think and what happens around you as you journal. You can use the journal to analyze and detect unhealthy thought patterns and address them. It is important to identify cognitive distortions in behavior or thoughts to treat them. You then gain more control over your days and learn to shift from negativity to a more positive mindset. This applies to yourself and the people around you.

The journaling itself has to be done it the right manner to benefit you. Writing random things without any thought to it will not be very useful. For constructive journaling, you need to keep some things in mind. One aspect is that you should write in a space that is personal and free from any distractions. You need to write every single day and note down at least a few parts of each day. After you finish writing about your day, you need to give yourself a bit of time to reflect on it. This will help you to take notice of your train of thoughts and actions. You should also find a private place to store the journal so that you know no one else will be privy to it. The journaling is for your eyes and benefit. Keeping it secure will allow you to be more open in your writing. You can share the thoughts in your journal with your therapist, but you don't necessarily have to show it to them either. Don't feel obligated to share the journal with anyone else.

Things to keep in mind while journaling:

❖ Think about what you want to write in your journal. Write about what is going on in your life, what your goals are and what your thoughts are. Also, write about what you are trying to avoid or ignore as well.

❖ After you write you need to take some time to reflect on the entry. Stay calm and take a few breaths.

❖ Use your writing to understand your thoughts and feelings. Take time and stop if you feel like you don't know what to write. Take a breath and start again.

❖ Try to set some time aside to write every day. Make sure you stick to writing for that much time.

❖ After your done, take a moment to reflect on everything you wrote and understood from your entry. Sum up your experience for that day in a sentence or two. Try to think of how you can do better next time.

Tips for journaling:

These tips will help you get started with journaling.

- Try writing as soon as you wake up or right before you go to sleep.
- Always try to be honest to yourself in your journal. You don't need to hide anything or filter your thoughts because the journal is for your eyes only.
- To get started, describe what you did the whole day. You can write about what you saw, what you thought, and even what happened to others around you. There is never any lack of things to write about.
- When you want to deal with your negative feelings or feel like you need a boost, try affirmations. These are sentences that you use to write positive things about yourself, and they boost your self-esteem. You need to develop a healthy sense of self-worth.
- Try writing about the people or things in your life that you are grateful for. You can write about something good that happened that day and how grateful you were for it. It can be some kind words or a gesture of kindness from others

or just anything that you are thankful for in general.

❖ Write about your dreams and goals and what you are doing to achieve them.

❖ Be your own critic in your journal but rationally and healthily. If you feel like you did something wrong, then analyze it and think of how you can do better.

❖ You can write about how you did at work or in any activity you took part in. Journaling can help you think about how you can do better and notice what you need to improve.

❖ You get a free zone to express your fears and anxiety. You can write about them and try to get to the source of this anxiety as well.

❖ Use your journal as a log of all the success you achieve. Mark down all the progress you make every day in dealing with your emotions, behavior and mental health.

A lot of research has shown that journaling is effective in helping people deal with stress, anxiety, and depression. It helps people with mental illness to identify their symptoms and accept their emotions. Journaling helps in easing the symptoms related to mental illness and improve quality of life. This simple practice also impacts the physical well being as it helps to deal with stress and related effects on the body. Also at the end of the day before going to bed, journaling will even help to improve your sleep cycle.

Does journaling help to treat depression?

The answer is definitely yes. It has been seen that journaling helps in managing symptoms of depression in people. Including journaling as a part of CBT helps to improve the results of the treatment. It is not effective singularly but combined with other tools for treatment, it is known to be very effective.

Studies have shown that writing has helped women who suffer from depression due to abusive relationships. It also helps adolescents who suffer from depression and are at risk for destructive behavior. Although journaling may not decrease how often automatic thoughts come into the mind, they help in limiting their impact. Journaling helps to reduce symptoms of depression like rumination as well. Research showed that those with major depression saw their depression scores lower within a few days of journaling. The overall benefit of journaling is quite clear. It allows you to release emotions, stay in a positive frame of mind, and build a buffer for negative thoughts.

Journaling can also help you through the process of recovery. If you have experienced a traumatic event, it can help to find good in every day. Writing your everyday experiences can make you find the positive aspects of your life and deal with the side effects of your trauma. For people that have eating disorders, it can be a relieving and healing method. It helps to limit obsessing over certain things and confront issues in a more head-on way. Journaling helps those with mental illnesses to stop ruminating and free their minds in a way that they can cope with the stress or anxiety bothering them. It can also help you to deal with the loss of a loved one. Expressing your emotions in a journal helps to process the loss and even prevent some maladaptive symptoms of coping that might arise. Children, who have to deal with bereavement, find this practice particularly helpful. The most important role in recovery played by journaling is in case of addiction. Addicts find that journaling helps them in their struggle against addiction. It allows them to also keep a record of their struggles as well as their accomplishments. They get a chance to hold themselves accountable for their actions and find a way to express their thoughts. The recovery from addiction can be a particularly hard process if the addict does not learn to control their thoughts and emotions healthily.

When you write down your thoughts and actions, it helps you to solidify your experiences and sense of self. You get a chance to reflect on what you have done and learn more about yourself every day. A journal allows you the chance to create a narrative for your own life. You realize that all the choices you make and your memories from the past together make you who you are. Journaling has a cathartic benefit on recovery.

Gratitude

One of the tools, which you can use while journaling, is cultivating gratitude. Gratitude is a very positive practice and is effective in helping people reach their goals as well as improving their life. Writing is one of the easiest ways to express gratitude.

- ❖ Gratitude helps to improve your well being in the long term.
- ❖ It helps to improve the quality of your sleep cycles.
- ❖ It helps in making you more optimistic and focuses on health and happiness.
- ❖ Gratitude journaling is effective in treating depression symptoms.
- ❖ Gratitude helps in improving your attitude towards people and life in general. Instead of antisocial tendencies, it promotes pro-social behavior.

Benefits of journaling:

If your in need of further convincing about the benefits of journaling, these will help you:

1. Journaling encourages and improves creative abilities.
2. It helps you to set goals and bring them to life.
3. It allows you the chance to get relief from stressors and let go of things that are not important.
4. It helps you to identify and explore your emotions or feelings.
5. You get a chance to write down the pros and cons of certain actions or decisions, helping you to reduce stress in your life
6. You will learn to pay attention to things that you previously might have ignored. This includes patterns of negativity in your behavior or thinking.
7. You will notice what factors influence your thoughts and actions every day.
8. Journaling allows you to channel all your emotions into words and thus release tension that can get pent up without expression.
9. Journaling can help you to discover your voice and improve writing skills.

10. You get a chance to keep a written record of your life that will be one of your precious keepsakes in the future.
11. You will see an increase in the sense of gratitude and learn to appreciate the good things in your life.

Precautions while journaling:

- ❖ Although journaling is a very helpful practice, don't think about it too much.
- ❖ Don't let the practice of writing about your life make you a passive observer of it.
- ❖ Don't use it to blame yourself for everything that happens. The aim is to find solutions to problems and not blame.
- ❖ Don't let it be a self-obsessive practice of writing about yourself.
- ❖ Don't focus on all the negativity in your life in your journal.

I hope all this information helps you to understand the benefits of journaling and encourages you to try it alongside your CBT therapy. If it is practiced the right way, it can lead to positive outcomes in your life and for your mental health. Don't let your journaling become an escape from the real world and start focusing on it obsessively.

Use it as a reflective tool that allows you to record your days and emotions. The benefits of journaling are far more than any disadvantages the practice could have. Use the tips given above to go about it the right way. You will see that it helps a lot in reducing stress and anxiety from your daily life.

Chapter 7

MINDFULNESS MEDITATION

Mindfulness meditation is yet another practice that is found to help in the treatment of mental illness along with CBT. It works as an additional tool that helps the individual improve the quality of their lives and attain real mental peace. The practice of meditation has been carried out for centuries and for good reason.

Mindfulness meditation is a type of training that teaches your mind to focus on what you are experiencing in the present moment. Instead of thinking of the past or future, you learn to live in the present. It teaches you to block out all the unnecessary chatter around you and also inside your mind. You learn to focus on things that matter singularly. This mental training practice involves breathing exercises, imagery, relaxation of the body and mind, and increased awareness as well.

The purpose of mindfulness meditation is to teach the individual to be more present in the now and increase awareness. The practice helps in the treatment of stress, anxiety, depression, insomnia, and other mental health issues. There are many ways to learn this practice. You can do it yourself through self-help programs or find a teacher to guide you. It is quite simple and can easily be included in your everyday routine. A few minutes every day to start with will make a difference.

- ❖ Start with finding a quiet and distraction-free area in your home.
- ❖ Sit in a comfortable but straight posture. Don't be stiff.
- ❖ Put aside thoughts of the past or future. Focus on the present.
- ❖ Start paying attention to your breathing. Focus on the movement of inhaling and exhaling. Notice how the air enters through your nose and let it out through your mouth. Practice this breathing exercise and focus on it.
- ❖ Don't try to control the thoughts that come into your head. Let them come and go. You

don't have to think about them or ignore them. Just be a bystander and watch these thoughts pass as you keep breathing.

❖ If you start getting distracted to think of something else, slowly bring your focus back to your breathing. Don't get anxious about the distraction, notice it but come back from it.

❖ Meditate for as long as you want to or can. Before you get up, slowly bring your focus to the present surroundings.

This meditation practice has many advantages for your mental as well as physical wellbeing. However, there is no mandatory guideline for instilling this into our life. You can meditate in an open park if you don't want to sit in the corner of your house. You also don't have to sit and meditate as we explained. You can choose to find some time that will allow you to be alone with your thoughts without being disturbed. In all the daily activities that you perform every day, it is easy to multitask and use this time for some mindfulness.

Try to Pay attention to the task you are performing, how you are feeling and the ground beneath your feet. This can be while you brush your teeth or even clean your house. Instead of watching videos while exercising, use this time to quietly move. Pay close attention to your movements and your breath and how your body feels. Turn off any sounds around you. These are simple ways to include mindfulness in your activities.

Mindfulness-integrated Cognitive Behavior Therapy

Let us now look at the application of mindfulness in CBT. You now have a simple idea of what mindfulness is and how you can implement it in your daily life. Here you will learn how it helps in the treatment of mental conditions along with CBT. Many psychological disorders can be treated using mindfulness integrated cognitive behavior therapy or MCBT.

It teaches you to pay attention to everything going on in your mind and around you in the present without being judgmental. You learn to be accepting and not react to every single thing that happens unless you need to. Mindfulness helps in countering the effects of stress or anxiety and helps you get detached to an extent. MCBT aims to help you see things as they are. Mindfulness also teaches you the reality of impermanence. You learn to accept that everything changes including your thoughts. It helps you to detach yourself from any bad habits or rigid views. These can cause unhappiness in your life, but mindfulness helps you detach from these elements.

MCBT involves four steps in its therapeutic approach to heal people. It integrates mindfulness with the principles of CBT to improve the way people think and behave. The approach is just a little different from what normal CBT entails. MCBT can help people in learning how to control the processes that cause unrealistic thoughts or beliefs in their minds. CBT by itself tries to change the behavior by changing the thoughts and beliefs. The process of thinking itself is changed using MCBT.

1. The first stage teaches mindfulness skills that help you to take note of unhelpful thoughts or emotions and let go of them. This is done for the person to successfully deal with the challenges life throws at them. The first stage of MCBT will teach you equanimity and help in developing deep insight so that you don't fall prey to all the negative thoughts that enter your mind.

2. The second stage allows you to implement the skills taught in the first stage. You will have to face situations that you would probably avoid normally, and this will help in increasing your confidence levels.

3. The third stage teaches you to improve interpersonal understanding and develop better communication skills. This will help you in situations where you might normally feel tense or cornered. You will learn not to react just because someone provokes you either.

4. The fourth stage teaches you to empathize with yourself. You need to learn to be kind to yourself and also to others. This empathy has to

be visible in what you do every day. It will improve your sense of worthiness and also improve your relationship with others. It is important to develop a caring nature and connect with others.

MCBT also helps in changing unhelpful coping strategies by using exposure as well as desensitization principles. According to the principles of this therapy, the reactive habits of a person are due to their reaction habits to body sensations. These body sensations develop from the way we think and learn to react to certain sensations to feel better. These habits usually develop since an early age and stick, as we grow older. MCBT helps in preventing these conditioned reactions but increasing awareness and acceptance of these experiences. This helps in changing habitual behavior and even feelings that arise in us. Thus, the therapy helps in providing emotional relief.

Other than changing their thoughts and behavior, MCBT also helps people to improve their relationships with those around them. It helps them to be more compassionate and accepting of others as they learn to be kinder to themselves. This helps in the development of harmonious relationships with people who will support and help you from relapsing into negativity again. The third phase of the therapy deals with this aspect of interpersonal mindfulness. The fourth stage teaches people to make use of the skills they learn and empathize with others as well as themselves. The last stage of the process sees the person become much more empowered and accepting of their emotions, situations, and the people around them. The duration of the entire program will depend on the individual and their needs.

Chapter 8

DEALING WITH NEGATIVE THINKING AND SELF-TALK

Negative thinking causes people to anticipate the absolute worst in every situation or circumstance. The negative thoughts that rooted from this type of thinking are not favorable for what that person needs or wants. Such people think of the negative aspect of everything. For instance, even if they like dogs, they think about the mess they would make and decide not to keep one. They know that a dog is loving and would make them happy, but they ignore this positive aspect and focus on the little things that might bother them.

Negative self-talk is a manifestation of this type of negative thinking. Some people will usually have a habit of expressing their negative thoughts or feelings in a way that it demotivates them from doing anything productive or good. They are constantly criticizing themselves and lack self-compassion. It's like they have a small voice inside their head that always tries to put them down. This voice can be very convincing and makes the person think that all the self-criticism makes sense. Even if they do one single thing wrong, they think they can't do anything right at all. They will convince themselves that they are not good at something or can't do something right. Instead of trying to do better next time and staying optimistic, they believe that their worst fears will always come true.

Negative self-talk can have negative consequences in your life:

- ❖ It makes you convince yourself that you cannot do something. The more you tell yourself this, the more you believe it even if it is not true. '
- ❖ You strive for perfection, and nothing less than that will suffice. A single mark makes things completely bad. There is either black or white and no gray area in between.
- ❖ Negative self-talk is also linked to depression and can aggravate it. Constantly putting yourself down can make the symptoms of

depression more prominent and damaging for your mental health.
- ❖ The impact of negative thinking and self-talk is quite immediate in your life:
- ❖ It will make you feel worse than you are already feeling.
- ❖ It will also be a blockade that will prevent you from getting what you want in life.

Types of negative thinking:

Negative thinking can come in many forms, and all of them are harmful for your wellbeing.

- ❖ The all-or-nothing type of thinking makes you feel like a complete failure even if you get a small thing wrong or everything is not perfect to your level.
- ❖ The attitude of disqualifying the positive aspects of situations and claiming life to be all bad.
- ❖ Negative self-labeling that makes you put yourself down constantly with derogatory terms or sentences.

- ❖ A catastrophizing attitude that makes you decide that everything will go wrong even if there is a small incident.
- ❖ They think that they can read minds and assume that they know what others are always thinking.
- ❖ The habit of using "should" statements, which deem that you should do something or someone else should do something. Such people can be very judgmental if people don't do what this person thinks they should.
- ❖ Need approval from others all the time.
- ❖ Disregarding the present and thinking of the past or future all the time.
- ❖ Many people have a negative, pessimistic attitude where they are never happy with things and always look at the negative aspect. In the glass half full and half empty categories, they fall in the latter.

All these negative types of thinking have an even worse impact when the negative thoughts keep replaying in your head, and you can't seem to control them. This can lead to stress, anxiety, and depression in most people. This is why it is important to recognize and identify those negative thoughts and push it in a more positive direction.

Effect of negative thinking:

Negative thinking can have a lot of impact on your mind, emotions, behavior, and life in general. It affects you and also the relationship you have with others.

- ❖ It does not allow you to lead the worthwhile life that you deserve.
- ❖ It causes low self-esteem and lack of self-confidence.
- ❖ It decreases the joy and happiness in your life and casts a shadow on it.
- ❖ It makes you feel weak instead of strong.
- ❖ Negative thoughts are a hindrance to success and pull you down.
- ❖ They affect the clarity of your mind and affect your ability to make decisions or think clearly.

It is important to appreciate yourself and your life to be happy. If you allow negative thinking to control you, you lose your chance at a happy life and peace of mind. Negative thinking is at the core of the problem of most mental disorders. It is in your best interest to start focusing on changing this negative train of thought that does not benefit you. It is important to work on being more optimistic and having constructive thoughts instead of destructive thoughts.

Changing your belief system

Some choose to persist in the face of failure while others choose to give up. Some decide to focus all their attention and effort on achieving the goals they set for themselves while others wander. Think of what drives these people and what makes people stay happy even in the face of despair. The answer to this is their belief system. They will react to different circumstances and situations according to their beliefs. Most people have beliefs that are rooted deep in their psyche, and this has developed since their formative years. It is fine if this belief system is positive, but some others have a more negative psyche that needs to be changed. But is it possible to change such a deep-rooted part of someone's mind? The answer is yes.

Let's look at some simple examples. When you sit in a chair, what makes you so sure that it won't break, and you won't fall? Some beliefs are so instilled in us that we don't even notice them, but they are a part of us. When you have a negative mindset, it creates negative beliefs. This is not constructive for you and affects your mental health. This is why it is important to change this kind of belief system. You need to start questioning your belief in all the negative self-talk and negative outcomes that you predict. "What if I won't fail?" "What if people like me?" These kinds of questions need to be asked and thought about rationally instead of beating yourself up about it. Don't create a negative certainty in your mind about everything. Questioning and instilling uncertainty in this negative belief system will be key to changing to a more positive mindset. This will help you grow as an individual and succeed in life. A negative belief system will only hold you back and aggravate mental instability. Thinking in affirmatives is important for a positive attitude.

How to stop negative thoughts and negative self-talk

It is important to create a bridge to positive thinking to defeat negativity. If you want to attract positive things, then you need to put out positive thoughts into the universe as well, this is known as the law of attraction. Negativity only breeds more negativity, and thinking like this will only attract negative events in your life. The important thing to take away from this is that you create your circumstances according to your thoughts and behavior. If you focus on the negative aspects of everything, then you lose sight of the positivity. Your thoughts can act like a magnet to achieve what you want in life. Thinking positively and acting positively will pull positivity towards you as well.

❖ When you see that negative thoughts come into your mind, don't let them overpower or overwhelm you. Try to stop this stream of negativity before it controls you.

❖ Use positive affirmations to get rid of negative thinking. Use positive sentences to reaffirm good thoughts. If you work hard for a test, use affirmative sentences to tell yourself that you will pass due to this effort. Don't stress out and think of how you might fail. Getting anxious will be a hindrance in concentrating and writing the test. This applies to any other instance as well. Use these positive affirmations to instill more self-confidence as well. Shift from self-criticizing and focus on empowering yourself. Believing in yourself is crucial to achieve what you want in life.

❖ Try writing negative thoughts or emotions on a paper and afterwards destroy the paper. If you feel emotions like jealousy or fear, express those in writing, and it will help you release the tension. Then destroy the paper and symbolize the end of the negativity.

❖ Use reasoning to change negative thinking. Evaluate a thought and rationalize it. Does your rationalization support a positive or negative outcome? Often, there are more chances of good things happening than bad things.

Feeling positive inside will help to bring positivity in our lives. You will attract what you are, so try being positive. If you think of good things, you will start appreciating the good that is already present in your life. Negative thinking does not allow you to take the positives in your life into consideration. All the negative self-talk will cloud your vision and look at your weaknesses instead of harnessing your strengths. It is normal for everyone to have a shortcoming, but there is so much more than you should focus on. Establishing a positive belief system can play an essential role in your life. Try meditation to help in this change. Starting talking in the positive and not negative. Question the negative thoughts and turn them into positives.

Chapter 9

REDUCING STRESS

Are your work hours too long? Do you feel too tired to spend quality time with your family or friends? Do you feel stuck in a situation? Does it feel like all your plans fail? This is a negative way of thinking that causes stress. Some people learn to identify the problem and deal with it appropriately. Others keep worrying and try to push the problem away instead of resolving it. Stress can have a very negative impact on our mind, body, and life in general. Negative thoughts can increase the stress level and make it more overwhelming. Most people in this day and age will deal with stress in some form or the other. If you ask your grandparents about their youth, you will probably find that their lives were much more stress-free when you compare them to yours. However, this does not take away from the fact that you do have to deal with a lot of stress in your life.

Many reasons can be the cause of your stress, such as:

- ❖ Problems in relationships.
- ❖ Financial issues.
- ❖ Challenging work environment.
- ❖ Medical conditions like a chronic illness.
- ❖ Prominent changes in your life.
- ❖ The death of a loved one.
- ❖ Emotional issues like depression or anxiety.
- ❖ A traumatic experience.
- ❖ Low self-esteem.
- ❖ Situations that you are not comfortable with like speaking in public.

All of the above are common causes of stress in the daily lives of most people. However, there are other reasons that we might not have listed but are just as valid.

Symptoms of stress:

Stress can be seen in the form of various symptoms in different people. Some of them include headaches, lack of appetite, binge eating, worrying, lack of concentration, change in sleeping patterns, stomach ulcers, high blood pressure, migraine, etc. These are just a few of the commonly seen symptoms in people suffering from stress. Other than these, it can also aggravate physical issues and affect your immunity. Stress can play a significant role in how you deal with an illness and affect your treatment as well. Nearly everyone is affected by stress in some way or the other. The difference is how they deal with it. Some learn to deal with their stress appropriately, but most get overwhelmed with it, and this affects their life. You need to learn to identify your stressor and see if it is something you can control or not. The key is to try to work with the things that are within your control and change it positively so that you are not faced with more stress. For situations out of your control, acceptance is key.

One of the main things you have to remember is that negative thoughts play a significant role in your mind and any stressful situation. The more negatively you think, the more stressed out you get. This can make your irritable and behave irrationally as well. Your negativity and stress will not just impact you but the people around you and your relationship with them.

One of the main aims of cognitive therapy is to change this way of thinking.

Benefits of CBT for stress:

- ❖ It will help you understand why some situations trigger stress responses in you.
- ❖ You will learn how some of your thinking and behavioral patterns prevent you from feeling good.
- ❖ CBT will teach you how to change your way of thinking or behaving so that you can get rid of the stressors in your life and also learn to cope with situations you cannot control.
- ❖ You will be more confident about dealing with stressful situations in your present and future.

CBT has been effective for treating severe stress and anxiety for many people. Cognitive and behavioral therapy can help you manage and improve your state of mind and deal with the stress in a better way. Your therapy will depend on how long you have been dealing with stress, your level of confidence, and the intensity of the situations that stress you out. CBT emphasizes that the stress will affect you depending on how you think in certain circumstances. For instance, if your flight gets delayed, you can have two kinds of responses to this. The first will be where you don't think too much about it and listen to some music or catch up on your emails. The other response will be where you think of the delay and your time getting wasted and feel distressed in the situation.

As you can see that your thought pattern will either give you a stressful response to a situation or allow you to stay calm. There are some common cognitive distortions like these that therapists help patients learn to deal with. They help them to identify the common stress triggers and change their thought pattern more positively so that they can stay calm in such situations.

If your situation is not too complex, then six sessions of therapy are most commonly prescribed by the therapist. If you have issues like low self-esteem and anxiety along with the original cause of stress, then the therapist might recommend at least 12 sessions of therapy. Those who have been suffering from stress for a very long time are usually advised to continue for more than 24 sessions and take as long as needed to treat the illness.

CBT works in resolving stress issues by helping people achieve some goals or changes. They can decide to change the way they act like becoming more outgoing instead of waiting for others to approach them. They can try to regulate their feelings and not get overwhelmed with fear or anxiety. CBT also teaches them to solve problems and get rid of thoughts that are self-defeating. It also helps them to deal with issues related to physical illness. Therapists using this process focus on helping the patients to deal with their present and not think of the past. Instead of just their personality, CBT therapists study their thoughts and beliefs to help them.

Compared to many other types of therapy, CBT has been seen to be much more helpful and shows faster results. Many studies have been conducted to compare the results of people being treated with CBT and other types of therapy. The positive results from the research on this therapy have made it a popular approach for most people. If you want to try CBT for treating stress then find a good therapist who will suit your needs.

How to make your life less stressful?

1. Start by making time for yourself. You might think that your week is too busy, and you don't have time to relax, but you need to set some time aside for yourself where you have no obligations. Use time management skills to schedule your work and other obligations to stay organized and on track. Take a break in between it all and do something relaxing like going for a walk or a swim. A good rest will help you perform all your tasks better. It will also help you feel better.

2. Prioritize and let go of the tasks that are not important. Identify your capacity and take on work accordingly. Taking on more than you can handle will ultimately cause stress. If you have a lot of work piled up, create a list and start with the priorities. Go according to the list so

that you know that the main objectives were dealt with. Focus on what is more important.

3. Start practicing assertive communication. If you feel like you are being taken advantage of in any relationship, you need to be better at communication. Don't be passive or aggressive but try to find a way to be assertive so that you can put your thoughts and needs forward firmly. People are more responsive to assertive behavior, and it puts forward a clear picture of what you need and feel. Assertive people are respected and respectful. You don't have to be passive to please others and increase your stress levels, but your behavior is important.

4. You need to realize that stress also takes a toll on your body and not just your mind. Try to practice some meditation or breathing exercises every day. Deep breathing is a great way to help your body calm down.

5. Pay attention to your thoughts. Don't let your thoughts get carried away when you get stressed about something. Stop and analyze whether you are being rational and think of something

calmer. If you can't find anything that supports your negative train of thought, then accept that it is unrealistic, and you should stop stressing over it.

6. Monitor your moods. CBT exercises for stress management use mood monitoring as a way to recognize negative thought patterns and challenge it. In this exercise, you have to write about a stressful event, how you felt about it, and rate it from 1 to 100 according to how stressful it was for you. Keep this paper and look at it the next day and assess the situation and your reaction. You will be out of that immediate stressful haze to be able to realize what was stressful and what you could do about it instead of worrying about it.

If you find the right therapist or CBT course, you will find it much easier to deal with stressful situations in the future. You will feel more at ease and get better at handling all kinds of situations. This will allow you to stay as stress-free as you can and even avoid most stressful situations in the first place.

Chapter 10

HYPNOTHERAPY

Hypnotherapy is a type of guided hypnosis that is conducted by clinical hypnotherapists to induce a trance-like state. The state induced using this hypnotherapy allows the person to be so focused and concentrated as though they are completely absorbed in some book and cannot listen to anything else. This hypnotic state allows the person to focus inside him or her and find a way to get better. This form of therapy is often used to treat stress or help the patient to break bad habits and many other problems. It is used for a variety of different applications, but it is difficult to assess how effective it is. This hypnotic state is induced to change behavior patterns and help the person find motivation within themselves.

Victorian hypnotists like James Braid practiced the traditional form of hypnotherapy. They used it to directly suggest the patient to remove symptoms like drug abuse or alcohol abuse. Milton H. Erickson developed a different approach to this hypnotism in the 1950s, and this was later known as Ericksonian hypnotherapy. He used informal conversation with therapeutic strategies and complex language patterns in this form of hypnotherapy. However, it was very different from the traditional way so many people questioned its validity as hypnotism.

The early 2000s saw the development of Ericksonian hypnotherapy being combined with solution-focused brief therapy that was goal focused. Then came cognitive-behavioral hypnotherapy or CBH. This uses CBT with clinical hypnosis for greater effectiveness of treatment. This integrated treatment showed a lot of improvement in patients who tried it.

Theodore X. Barber and some of his colleagues published a review of research on this in 1974. They argued that hypnotism was not a special state but a culmination of psychological variables like active imagination and motivation. As more research was done, cognitive as well and behavioral theories were used to explain hypnosis, and this allowed more integration of hypnotherapy with CBT.

Curative hypnotherapy was originated from the work of David Lesser, and thus it is called Lesserian therapy. He understood the possibility of using hypnosis with IMR and questioning to find the causes behind the symptoms of patients. He did not focus on directly trying to push on subconscious information but worked on developing a process to correct wrong information. His work emphasized on the simplicity and logic of the subconscious mind and helped in the creation of the present-day treatment.

As more work and study is done to understand the subconscious, the therapy keeps evolving. The Trance Theory of Mental Illness was put forward by Dr. Peter Marshall. According to this, people who suffer from any neurosis like depression are already living in a state of trance, and it does not have to be induced. Instead, they need to understand the state they are in and the hypnotherapist has to help them come out of it.

Hypnotherapy can be used with CBT to treat many psychological issues like depression, anxiety, substance abuse, phobias, etc. It is used to help people in improving their sleep patterns, communication issues, behavioral problems, and many such related conditions. It is also used for aiding in pain management and resolving medical conditions. Dentists might use hypnotherapy to help patients deal with their fear or treat oral conditions like teeth grinding.

Hypnotherapy is not used as a therapy itself but as an aid with CBT. Finding trained and certified health care professionals for hypnosis is important. The patient should find a hypnotherapist that is qualified but also someone they can resonate with and be comfortable for therapy.

Cognitive Hypnotherapy is a combination of hypnosis with CBT using theories of neuroscience. The natural state of mind that we often find ourselves immersed in like while we read a book or listen to music is the state that is used for therapy in cognitive hypnotherapy. You are not put under someone's control or put into a state where you are helpless. It is just an effective method of helping you to make positive changes. This form of therapy is usually conducted only for a couple of sessions and allows the patient to feel at ease.

Misconceptions about Hypnotherapy:

Hypnosis or hypnotherapy is attached to many misconceptions.

- ❖ Some people think that gullible or uneducated people are the only ones who fall prey to hypnosis. They think that being subjected to hypnosis makes a person more gullible. However, this is not true. Hypnosis can only be done when the participant is willing, regardless of how educated or intelligent they are.
- ❖ It is a misconception that is commonly thought hypnosis to be a state where the person is asleep or unconscious. It is a state of altered consciousness. It is similar to being focused singularly on an activity and not paying

attention to anything else. The state achieved by meditation is similar to a hypnotized state.

❖ There is a misconception that hypnosis can be performed against a person's will and can cause you to reveal secrets. This is not true because hypnosis or hypnotherapy does not involve mind control. The person is always in control and will be able to tell if they are being made to do something they are uncomfortable with.

❖ You don't have to worry about staying stuck in a hypnotic state. People always come out of the hypnotized state at some point. If they don't willingly come back to reality, they might fall asleep and come back to their normal state. No one stays stuck in hypnosis forever.

❖ People also think that hypnosis can make your mind weaker, but this is not true either. It does not make the person susceptible to the hypnotist's control.

❖ It is a myth that hypnosis will make you remember everything from your childhood.

❖ Hypnosis does not necessarily need another hypnotist or hypnotherapist. It can also be self-induced and is called self-hypnosis. It is a skill that can be learned with time and experience.

❖ There is no single way to enter into a hypnotic state. There are different responses from different people, and each is equally valid.

❖ Hypnosis is sometimes confused with meditation, which is something that it is not. Meditation is a method of relaxing as the person tries to empty their mind from all thoughts. Hypnosis is induced to achieve something in particular.

Chapter 11

Focusing on the Future

Getting Rid of Toxic Connections

The people in your daily life play a major role in it and your mental health as well. Some people in your life will be uplifting and supportive, and you should keep them around and return the favor. However, there are many more that are toxic connections that need to be severed.

Take a second and think of the people you are always around. Think of that friend you have been friends with for years. Do you notice that she criticizes you far more than she encourages you? Think of the co-worker you hang out with. Have you noticed that he never uses your ideas or praises you in front of others? Your partner can also be someone who constantly puts you down when he should be one of your main sources of support.

Start analyzing your relationships and pick out the weeds that are hindering your growth. This is an important aspect of ensuring your happiness and success. Toxic people will only take from you and have nothing good to contribute to your lie.

If you have a mental illness, you might not have paid attention to this aspect before. But its important to recognize the fact that the people around you also contribute to your mental health and wellbeing. If they are manipulative, aggressive, narcissist or have any such negative tendencies, this is something that will also affect you. You might have known these people your whole life and don't know what to do. It might be a little easier to cut off someone who just entered your life but those who have been around a long time are a little harder to get rid of.

Even though they make you feel bad, you don't know how to sever this connection. However, some people are better at dealing with such toxic people. They recognize the negative impact from this kind of toxic behavior and know how to deal with them. They can either cut them off or learn to not let them affect their lives. People with low self-esteem or lack of confidence will have a hard time doing this. But people with a stronger mental state will be better at managing toxic relationships.

If you need help in managing toxic relationships, here are some tips that will assist you.

Assess situations where you felt rail-roaded by someone. Before shifting the blame on someone else for making you feel bad, reflect on yourself. Do you allow them to talk over you because you fear confrontation or don't have confidence? Think of encounters with these people and try to assess your emotions and actions at the time. What was the reason behind your action and why did you allow the toxic person to make you a victim of their spite? Pay attention to how you react in situations to understand yourself.

Now think about your reactions in situations. Did you react appropriately or overreact or maybe did not react enough? Anyone studying your reactions to another person will be able to make out the dynamic in that relationship. There can be some people in your life who have bullying or narcissistic tendencies. This dynamic is often found in abusive relationships. If you don't react properly to mistreatment and let it slide, it allows the person to think they can continue to behave that way. This is a case of under reaction that causes the situation to escalate. A narcissist will love playing games with an insecure person. An insecure person will fall prey to their games and overreact if they feel like they might lose their relationship with the narcissist. This is because an unhealthy and insecure attachment is in place. This overreaction makes the narcissist feel powerful and reinforces the same cycle.

To deal with these kinds of reactions, it is necessary to learn to manage your emotions. Think over these situations and plan on how you will react the next time. Set some goals to see changes and improve the dynamics in your relationships. Focus on a scenario and think of what you will do when it arises the next time. Think of the words that you should say to make the person realize that you are taking control of yourself and will not allow them to treat you like a pushover. Assertive sentences and body language will help you in this. Standing up for yourself is important if you don't want to allow toxic people to undermine you.

It is also important to trust yourself. An insecure person will be more likely to stay in a toxic relationship. They don't trust themselves to be alone or trust their own judgment. They let the misbehavior of the other person pass by rationalizing that they did not mean it or any other such excuse. Instead of trusting their gut, they choose to give the other person the benefit of doubt. You need to stop making excuses for the misbehavior of others. Think about why you are allowing them to get away with it and try to get yourself out of that pattern. There is no valid rationalization for toxic behavior.

For some reason, all humans tend to hold on and do not like the idea of losing things. This applies to material things as well as the people in their lives. Dealing with any loss is avoided at all cost. However, if a person in your life has no positive contribution to it, is it really a loss? Should you not think of it as a long-term gain when you lose a toxic person? Many people will hold on to toxic relationships because they don't like to think of being alone or think that all their effort would go to waste if they gave up now. They can't think of what would happen after they got out of the toxic relationship because this is what they are familiar with. The fear of the unknown can be a strong factor. This kind of thinking creates an unconscious pattern where you stay stuck in a toxic relationship. Your mind tells you to hold on to something just because you have invested time and effort into it. Instead, you need to start focusing on what you will gain if you let go. The answer will be usually peace of mind and happiness. You will find yourself in a much better place if you get out of the toxic relationship of any kind. This can be your boyfriend, friend, work relationship, etc.

Being optimistic is an advantage. In an unhealthy state of mind, people tend to focus on the negativity and the bad outcomes possible. But in general, most humans are optimistic. They like to think that something good will eventually happen. This is seen easily when you look at people playing slot machines. They keep at it, in the hope that they might get lucky at some point. If you win once, you will keep trying a hundred more times to win one more time.

B.F. Skinner conducted an experiment of intermittent reinforcement. The apparatus included their rats in three cages. There were levers attached to all of the cages to deliver food to them. The first lever always delivered food to the rat so that rat got complacent and knew he would always have food. The second lever did not work, and this rat knew he would not be getting food from it. The third lever worked randomly and sometimes delivered food while sometimes it did not. This meant that the third rat knew that he might get food at some point even if he did not get it a couple of times, so his attention was always focused on the lever. This is intermittent reinforcement, and the same principle works for humans too.

In abusive relationships, it is seen that the abuser is usually mean, but he may also act extremely nice at times. The insecure person will focus on this good behavior and make excuses for bad behavior. They keep telling themselves that things will keep better, and the abuser will act well more often. However, this is not true and not enough reason to stick around. Don't search for scraps of kindness in a relationship that is destructive.

Set boundaries for relationships that cannot be cut off or avoided. This applies when you have family or friends that you will inevitably come in contact with at some point or the other. You know that these people always act negatively towards you and engage in unwarranted criticism but you probably never stood up for yourself. It is important to set boundaries with such people to protect yourself. Call them out if they are rude or inappropriate but not aggressively. Be assertive and display confidence in your manner. Most bullies stand down when they are faced with confidence. If someone crosses a limit at work, report him or her. If someone keeps commenting on how you look, let him or her know that they should not concern themselves about it. If someone makes jokes at your expense, don't go along with it to please others. Take a stand for yourself and let them know that it is not funny. A little sarcasm will do the trick without being directly rude in some cases. For those that you actually can get rid of, do it.

If you decide to stand up to toxic people, you also need to expect retaliation. Such people don't like to lose or feel out of control. If they see you taking control or setting boundaries, they might push harder. They will probably increase their efforts to bring the dynamics back to what they are comfortable with. This can include all sorts of manipulations, bad-mouthing or even physical violence. You need to anticipate and prepare for these types of retaliation. Stand firm and don't let them gain control over you again.

Don't close your eyes to bad behavior. Even if you have been in a toxic relationship for a very long time and are used to it, don't normalize it. Don't make excuses for the person who misbehaves or talks rudely all the time. Bad behavior is not excusable and is not something you should get used to. Don't rationalize someone's harsh words and tell yourself that it doesn't matter. Also, don't let another person ignore you or treat you like your opinion does not matter. This is another type of abusive behavior. Some liars make excuses when they are caught and try to push the blame on the innocent person. Even physically abusive people make excuses for their behavior by making the victim feel like they pushed them to it. Abuse is not okay whether it is emotional, verbal, or physical. Don't normalize this kind of behavior or allow yourself to get used to it. It is important to call them out and demand respect.

Toxic people make a habit of coming back into your life even when you try to cut them off. It is important to make sure that it is permanent. Don't allow the person to make excuses and try to push their way back into your life. No matter what they say, they will always create problems in your life. Move on from such toxic relationships for good. Treat such separations like a break-up. You know that some relationships have to end when they bring you more pain than happiness or if your partner cheats and lies to you. Let go of these people and don't allow them a chance to come back into your life. You will soon learn that you never needed them and are happier after the breakup.

A lot of toxic people try to act like they are vulnerable and need you around. The truth is that you don't need to be their savior. They are just being manipulative so that you excuse their bad behavior and stick around. They look for your time and attention by acting troubled. When you try to cut toxic people off, they try many different means to keep getting your attention. There can be some toxic friends who always look to you for help. But if you feel like it is overwhelming, then direct them towards someone who can help them. You are not responsible for another person's problems and do not need to burden yourself with them beyond your capability.

The more time that you spend away from toxic people, the more you will feel better. Surround yourself with positive and uplifting people. The energy flow around you will affect your own happiness. Staying around negative people and giving them power over you will only pull you down. If you can't break free of some toxic relationships, then learn to set firm boundaries with them. You need to talk yourself into being more assertive about what is okay with you and what that person needs to change as well. Don't allow people who are toxic to stay in your life and control you. Make time for those who bring you more happiness and work on being happier by yourself as well.

How to let go of the past and build the new you?

Learning to let go is an important step to move forward in your life. Letting go does not always mean that you have to get rid of something, but it means that you will let it be. It is no help to hold on to pain or replay the past in your mind over and over again. Things that happened in the past cannot be changed even if you wish for it. There is no reason to blame yourself and keep thinking of what you should have done either.

You have to accept what was and what is and let go. Change is inevitable and to accept it in a healthy manner, it is important to let go. You need to learn to let go of things or people that hurt you as well even if it seems hard. Holding on will prevent you from building a stronger and happier version of yourself. Who you become now will be defined by what you want to be and not by what you were. Your past is a part of your life, but it does not have to define you. Sometimes people get used to the pain and memories and choose to live in that comfortable zone of what they know. It can be intimidating to think of change, but it is necessary. Letting go can seem next to impossible for some people, but it isn't that hard. Here you will learn a few ways to let go and build yourself up.

1. You have to accept that things don't always go as planned and people don't always turn out to be the way we expected them to be. The relationship you have right now might be very different from what you had wanted or expected. Things rarely if ever, turn out to be as we expect them, and it is important to accept

this. Acceptance and gratitude will help you improve what you do have right now and make the best of it. You need to trust the process and hope that you will get where you want to be.

2. Try to keep a check on expectations from other people. Expecting too much from another person almost always ends in disappointment. Expectations make you fear the outcome of things not turning out as you want them to as well. There is no guarantee to how things can turn out or how someone will behave. You need to be more rational about dealing with expectations that are not met. Don't focus on them and learn to let go.

3. Don't limit yourself with negative self-talk. Let go of any inhibitions that don't allow you to move forward and achieve your goals. Keep an open mind and don't limit yourself when you are capable of so much more. The fear of failure can often stop people from even trying, but if you just let go of this fear, you will accomplish much more. Don't allow others to tell you what you can or cannot do either. Use their

discouragement as encouragement to prove such people wrong.

4. You need to let go of the notion that you have any control over someone else's actions. You can only control yourself and not another individual who is responsible for themselves. Don't waste your energy in trying to change a toxic person. They can only do this by themselves. Don't try to get affection and appreciation by doing more for others than you should be doing for yourself. Focus on changing yourself for the better and use your energy on yourself.

5. Stop worrying about what people think of you. Let go of these kinds of worries and think of yourself. Prioritize your feelings and opinions. If you constantly seek approval from others, it can be very pressurizing. Live by your values and don't focus on what others say or think about you.

6. Give yourself leeway for mistakes; you are only human. Let go of trying to be perfect. Use your mistakes to learn lessons. Don't berate yourself

over silly things and learn to let go of them. Your mistakes can be funny when you think about them later.

7. Let go of the things that you cannot change. Don't keep thinking of how things could have turned out. Be present in the now. If you want to live your life to the fullest, the present is where it is happening. You have no control over your past, but you can make the right decisions to make your future better.

8. Avoid getting too serious about every single thing. Relax and let some things go at their own flow. Learn to laugh some things off even if they aren't what you wanted or expected. It is all a part of your journey. Taking yourself too seriously will only cause stress and anxiety.

9. Let go of your fears as much as possible. It is human to fear things that can really harm us. But keeping too much fear within you will hold you back from a lot of experiences. Getting out of your comfort zone can be quite crucial at times. Fear will close off the possibilities of your life and block your mind from better thoughts.

Facing your fears will make you get over them. It will help you grow and succeed in life.

10. Be expressive about your thoughts and opinions. Use your voice to express yourself. Don't let others overshadow you or ignore your opinions. You matter just as much as anyone else and have the right to express yourself. Communication is also key to finding a good balance in relationships. If you bottle up your emotions, you allow the frustration to build up inside you. Getting things out makes it easier to deal with them right then. Even if you are angry about something, let the person know right then. If you hold back and keep all the anger inside, it will affect your relationship with that person quite badly. Expression is important for your own mental wellbeing and for better communication with others. Let go of your inhibitions about speaking up.

11. Bereavement or the loss of a loved one is one of the crucial times in your life. Death is inevitable and has to be accepted. Don't try to hold back your feelings at this time. Allow yourself to

process your emotions and grieve. There is no shame in crying and grieving. Being hurt or sad at such times is normal. Let go of the feelings and don't try to say strong by holding back. Grieving is a way to honor the dead as well.

12. Let go of grudges. It is important to learn to forgive people. You don't have to necessarily forget what someone did to you. Remembering will make your more cautious around them. But forgiving will help you move on. The forgiveness is beneficial for you and is not all about the other person. It will definitely make them feel better but don't hold on to grudges to punish them. Holding on to such feelings allows negativity to build up within you. Let go of feelings that hold you back in life and make you live in the past.

It is important to let go of things that hold you back in life. You need to move past what has happened and look towards the future. Holding on to any negative feelings or ideas about yourself will only harm you. These will come in the way of your personal growth and happiness. Stop trying to control everything and accept what is. Letting go of things will help you to learn more about life and yourself.

How to stay positive every day?

Positivity can be very beneficial for your health and happiness. This will only work if you practice it in your actions and thoughts every single day.

Firstly, you need to create the right kind of environment around you. This includes your physical environment and the people you surround yourself with. These factors have a huge effect on your life. Your environment should be conducive to the life you want to live. Surround yourself with people who want to do the same good things that you are trying to do. Find encouraging and supportive friends to hang out with. Join support communities when you are trying to bring a change like combating addictions. Read books or watch videos that are inspiring. Find someone who will hold you accountable for your actions at the end of your day. Make your space positive and filled with things that promote wellbeing. Clean up and keep things neat to make your mind feel the same way as well. A dirty and messy workspace or bedroom is a negative space to be in.

If you want to cultivate good habits in your life, start small. Don't over-do it and put pressure on yourself. Take things one by one and one day at a time. It will help you to incorporate a positive practice into your routine over time. Trying too much at once can be overwhelming and make you want to give up. Go at a pace that you can handle.

Take note of the positive things that happen, or you do every single day. Take a few moments at the end of the day to reflect on it. Your positive thinking will see a surge if you focus on the good. If you focus on the bad, you will build on a negative attitude. Writing or thinking about positive things will make you feel better and keep you in a better mood all day. You will also see that you sleep much better and have less stress levels. A gratitude journal can be helpful in this process.

Start meditating every day. Even if it is just for a couple of minutes in a day, it will make a difference. You have already seen how beneficial mindfulness meditation can be in your life. Meditation helps in improving focus, keeps your mind calm, and improves your mental as well and physical health. Just starting with two minutes in the morning will have a positive impact on your entire day. It will help you build good habits and see progress in your mental state.

Quick Fix Tips to stay Positive

- ❖ Life or circumstances can get hard at any point. In the face of this, it is important to stay positive and not let negative thoughts overwhelm you. I have shared a few effective habits that can help you stay positive in the face of such situations. I hope you find them useful.
- ❖ One of the most effective ways is to be optimistic in a negative situation. Even if you stumble upon some hardships, focus on the positive aspects of the situation and what you still have to be grateful for. Also look for a

window of opportunity that will help you make things better. This is a much better attitude than complaining about a bad situation. Don't force yourself to ignore the tough situation but take time to process the fact that there will usually be something that can work to your benefit in any situation.

❖ Try to cultivate a positive environment and surround yourself with the right kinds of people. Your company matters and should be chosen carefully. Bad company can have a bad influence on you. Find people who support you and contribute to your growth as a person. Take some time to think of the people who are negative influences in your life and distance yourself from them. Also, think of anything you do that has a negative impact on you and stop doing it.

❖ It is also important to pace yourself. Don't try to get things done in a rush, no matter what they are. This urgency can actually cause stress to build up and affect you. Slow down and take things into perspective as you go about your work. This will help you stay calm and go about things more constructively.

- ❖ Don't lose perspective and allow yourself to get stressed over unnecessary things. It is easy to imagine a huge problem arising even when there is a small one. If you find yourself panicking and thinking too much of a problem, try to stop and take a breath. Stop that train of thought and focus on your present as you take deep breaths. Change your focus to gain a wider perspective of the problem and try to find a solution calmly. Also, ask yourself if that same problem will matter in a few years and if you should be stressing over it.

- ❖ Don't let self-doubt hold you back from achieving success or happiness. If you want to get things done, you need to take a chance. Don't hold back because you fear you might fail. You might fail, but you might succeed as well so don't doubt yourself. Ask yourself what the worst scenario could be, and you will see that it is something that you will be able to handle. Don't let a vague fear control your actions and stop you from achieving what you want.

❖ Other than yourself, add positivity to others' lives as well. Giving is an important virtue that has to be harnessed. People will usually treat you how you treat them. Treat them with kindness and compassion, and they will usually do the same for you. Value your relationships with others, and you will see that they will benefit you. Help people if you see they need assistance. It could be in the form of the smallest gestures, but it will matter. You should smile at others more often, and you will see that it is infectious and makes a difference in their day. Be there for people when they need someone to talk to and listen.

❖ Regular exercise and a good diet are also important. Exercise helps in stimulating happy hormones and also keeps your body healthy. Good food is also important for you to feel good. Being lazy and eating junk food is a negative way to live and does not add quality to your life. Don't try starving yourself to lose weight either. Healthy regular meals will help in stabilizing your mood too.

- ❖ Accept healthy criticism. You don't have to fear criticism from other people. Listen and analyze what another person says. If it makes sense and will benefit you, pay attention to the criticism since it is constructive. If someone criticizes you out of spite, be the bigger person and ignore him or her. Also, don't take it to heart or allow it to affect your sense of self-worth. You don't have to immediately reply when someone criticizes you. Stay calm and listen. If it angers you, try taking a few deep breaths. Replying in the heat of the moment will only escalate the problem. Keep an open mind and consider that the criticism might work to your benefit. There is always room for growth for every person. Also, remember that what a person says is not just about you but also reflects on that person himself. Some people project their insecurity on others by using harsh words. Don't take it personally. When you reply to critics, be calm and collected. If it is just a malicious attack, you have to learn to let go for your benefit.

❖ Learn to let go of steam. If something affects you, don't try to suppress it. Learn how you can react to it better. Share the problem with another person that you trust and ask for their input. Also, work on building a strong sense of self-esteem so that things don't easily affect you or bring you down. Negativity should bounce off you and not get under your skin.

❖ Always try to start your day positively. This can mean making your bed, drinking some tea, practicing yoga, or doing meditation. Starting your day with meditation or exercise is actually a very positive method. It allows you to start your day with control and in a healthy way. You can also choose to listen to some good music or motivating podcasts to set the mood for the day. You will see that these will make a difference in how the rest of your day goes.

❖ Be mindful in your thoughts and actions throughout the day. Living in the present makes it harder for negative thoughts or emotions to overtake your thoughts. If you stay in touch with the present and practice positivity, you will see that it is easier to stay happy. If you get bored or start reminiscing, you might start to worry or get stressed again. This will not benefit your mental health. Go through your day at your own pace and be mindful in your actions so that you stay in the present. Try to focus your attention on whatever you are doing or wherever you are at that very moment. Use your senses to connect completely with the present.

All of these regular practices will help you stay positive and maintain a healthy mental state. Try to implement them consciously for a while, and you will soon see that they are a part of your lifestyle. Your negative habits will soon be replaced with these good habits. You need to remember that habits take time to develop so stay persistent in your efforts if you want to see real improvement in your mental health.

Relapse

A possibility of a relapse is always there, but it can be prevented or dealt with when the time comes. The skills learned during therapy will make it easier to control the symptoms of your anxiety or depression if they recur. Don't let go of the skills taught during therapy even if you feel like you are cured.

Maintaining mental health is a constant process. If you take your stability for granted, stressors might cause you to relapse into maladaptive behavior again. However, it is said that those who get treated through CBT have a lower chance of relapsing compared to those who were just treated through medication. If you feel like you can't help yourself, you can always seek guidance from your therapist again.

Chapter 12

PRECAUTIONS

Cognitive behavioral therapy can be very beneficial for you if you use it in the right way. Here I've enlisted some precautions to keep in mind when you decide to start CBT.

Many techniques are used while treating a person using CBT. It is important to choose the right technique that will help in dealing with your condition in particular. The correct diagnosis and treatment need to be used to see improvement. You need to remember that what works for one person does not necessarily work for another person. Each person has his or her own needs that have to be considered. The right technique needs to be chosen accordingly. Even if CBT does not work for you, you can always try another type of therapy like stress inoculation training. This might help you if CBT does not.

Other than choosing the right kind of therapy, it is also important to choose the right therapist. Just a degree is not enough to show that the person will help in treating your condition. Do some background checks and ask around about good therapists. The best testimonial to their work will be happy patients. Many online sources will help you find out about therapists and their work. Use it to your advantage and find the right fit for you. If you decide not to go to a therapist, you can even try online sources that help in therapy. Make sure you do good research on whatever form of therapy you choose or the therapist as well.

While choosing your treatment and therapist, consider what is feasible for you as well. Some centers or therapists may charge much more than you can or should spend. Choosing an exorbitantly expensive therapist will add to your bills and stress. Use your research to find someone who charges the appropriate rates and has good history with patients. This way you get your money's worth and don't burn a hole in your pocket. If you cannot afford a real therapist, there are

Internet therapy courses that will be more cost effective for you. Just find the right one and use it to your benefit.

You also need to remember that things take time. You cannot rush or lengthen the process, as you want. The therapy will last for different times for different people. You need to keep giving your maximum commitment to it to see results. Don't expect major changes in a day or even a week. Give it a couple of months and see how it works for you. If it really does not seem to be helping, then consider another form of therapy or therapist. Don't compare your progress with anyone else at any point. The whole point is to heal your mind, and if you want long-term benefits, then you cannot have short-term effort.

Although CBT is a great form of therapy, keep your expectations reasonable. It works differently for different people and different conditions. There won't be any overnight changes, and you will not become miraculously perfect in a week. Keep at it and watch the little things change and how CBT makes your mental health improve.

If you really want CBT to work for you, keep these precautions in mind.

Conclusion

As you come to the end of this book, I would first like to express my gratitude for choosing this as your source of information. I hope you have found this book informative about Cognitive Behavioral Therapy and that is it is useful to you. All the information has been assembled together after thorough research and put in a way to help you understand it better.

CBT has been recommended all over the world for treatment in mental illnesses due to its effectiveness. Therapists have stopped focusing singularly on drugs for treatment and use CBT for a much more thorough and personal approach towards treatment of mental health. It has been found to help people suffering from depression, personality disorders, behavioral problems and many other issues that are related to mental health.

You can always seek help and try this therapy to help you in healing from depression, anxiety, or any other mental issue you are facing. Giving importance to mental health is just as important as physical health. A healthy body will not be of much use if your mind is in a constant state of negativity. Try cognitive behavioral therapy and see how it helps you to deal with these issues and lead a much better life.